The Hippies and American Values

The Hippies

and American Values

TIMOTHY MILLER

The University of Tennessee Press ✱ *Knoxville*

Copyright © 1991 by
The University of Tennessee
Press / Knoxville.

All Rights Reserved.

Manufactured in the
United States of America.

Cloth: 1st printing,1991.
Paper: 1st printing,1991;
         2nd printing, 1992;
         3rd printing, 2000;
         4th printing, 2003.

This book is printed on acid-free
paper.

Library of Congress
Cataloging-in-Publication Data

Miller, Timothy, 1944–
    The hippies and American
    values / Timothy Miller.
        p.   cm.
    Includes bibliographical
    references and index.
    ISBN 0–87049-693-x
    (cl.: alk. paper)
    ISBN 0–87049-694-8
    (pbk.: alk. paper)
    1. Hippies—United States—
History. 2. Subculture—History.
3. United States —Social
conditions—1960–1980. I. Title.
HQ799.7.M55   1991
305.5'68—dc20   90-48062

FOR ABRAHAM *A Free Spirit*

Contents

Illustrations

Following page 84

Acknowledgments

Many persons helped bring this study to fruition. Those who deserve the most thanks are Norman Yetman, Stephen Fox, Robert Shelton, and Pam Detrixhe, all of whom read and commented on early versions of the manuscript; my sister Gretchen and her family; and my wife Tamara and our children, Jesse and Abraham. Roger Martin provided insights at crucial junctures, as usual. Lori Springs combed her collection for illustrations. Charley Shively and Janet Jacobs read later versions of the manuscript and made excellent suggestions which improved the book considerably. The library staff at the University of Kansas as usual provided timely, professional assistance. The Graduate School at the University provided funding for illustrations. Former hippies in Lawrence and elsewhere provided many pleasant hours of reminiscing that helped me to formulate my ideas. Eric Alstrom of Ann Arbor provided good and timely help in locating illustrations. Finally, the editors at the University of Tennessee Press are talented professionals; working with them has once again been a great pleasure.

CHAPTER I

Introduction

I am in effect setting up moral codes and standards which include drugs, orgy, music and primitive magic as worship rituals—educational tools which are supposedly contrary to our cultural mores; and I am proposing these standards to you respectable ministers, once and for all, that you endorse publically the private desire and knowledge of mankind in America, so to inspire the young.

—Allen Ginsberg, San Francisco *Oracle*, January 1967

On a sunny afternoon in the fall of 1967, at the end of the Summer of Love, a band of San Francisco hippies solemnly filled a coffin with stereotyped artifacts of hippiedom and burned it, pronouncing, as they did so, the "death of hip." Hip actually lasted at least two or three years longer before it succumbed to political violence, nihilism, and the crass commercialization of its ideas and values. However, although the four or five years that comprised the heyday of the counterculture passed into history nearly a quarter-century ago, a hippie legacy survives in America.

The hippies made a lasting impact on the ethos of America. The counterculture, in its broad-spectrum challenge to the prevailing culture, argued that America needed a sweepingly new ethics appropriate to an age characterized by never-ending global power struggles, technocracy, urbanization, environmental catastrophe, and psychedelic chemistry. The hippies saw themselves as the people of zero, the vanguard who would build a new society on the ruins of the old, corrupt one. They defined their task as bringing to the world a radical change of outlook—one which not only featured "new ideas" in some superficial sense (what politician does not claim to have new ideas?), but which constituted a fundamentally new way of getting at living, at seeing the world. The hippies were getting at root matters when, for example, they questioned the very rationality upon which Western culture has been built. To the counterculturists, reason had run its course; now it was time to return to the mystical and intuitional. The products of centuries of reason-dominated culture were thrown into question as well: the hippies rejected the industrial for the agrarian, the plastic for the natural, the synthetic for the organic. Finally they challenged the formidable Western tradition of setting the individual on a pedestal; for the hippies, communal values stood over the rights and privileges of individual persons.

From such basic questioning of received truth, the hippies began in a fragmentary, tentative way to outline a new ethics, born of the precepts of intuition and direct experience, often at odds with the values of the prevailing culture in the midst of which the counterculture found itself. Limning the outlines of that ethics is the task of this book.

Back in the days of hip a few observers realized that undergirding the emergence of a new, alternative lifestyle were some distinctively new values and ethical propositions. Among the first to notice were J. L. Simmons and Barry Winograd, who in 1966 discerned a "hang-loose ethic" in the then-emerging counterculture. They saw the main features of that ethic as irreverence, experience, and tolerance.[1] A few years later, William C. Shepherd probed the possibility of an important new ethical outlook when he observed that "if a code of ethics is said to be a necessary component of religion, the new youth culture, with its emphasis on honesty, integrity, gentleness, and personal freedom surely does have one, although it is vague and largely borrowed."[2]

As Shepherd suggested, the ethics of the hippies was never synthesized and promulgated in systematic form. Hip literature and culture, however, abounded with new ethical energy, and some of the more thoughtful hippies specifically proclaimed the existence of a grandly new ethics, systematic or no. Chester Anderson, for example, observed in 1968 that "It's the hippies who are developing an ethic and morality for an over-populated world; it's the hippies—ONLY the hippies—who are speaking to the youth of America."[3]

Most popular media coverage of the hippies focused on color and controversy—on be-ins, drugs, nudity, outlandish costumes, and the like. But amid the gawking a few of the more perceptive reporters saw deeper currents running in hippiedom. *Time*, for example, in a cover story on the hippies during the Summer of Love (1967), noted that a new ethical outlook was part of the hip presence:

> If there were a hippie code, it would include these flexible guidelines:
> —Do your own thing, wherever you have to do it and whenever you want.
> —Drop out. Leave society as you have known it. Leave it utterly.
> —Blow the mind of every straight person you can reach. Turn them on, if not to drugs, then to beauty, love, honesty, fun.[4]

And surprisingly (*Time* was, after all, an influential organ of the hated Establishment), the anonymous writer found that the counterculturists did a respectable job of trying to live their ideals: "Indeed, it could be argued that in their independence of material possessions and their emphasis on peacefulness and honesty, hippies lead considerably more virtuous lives than the great majority of their fellow citizens."[5]

Ethical innovation and commitment, yes; systematic analysis, no. Hip ethics, as proclaimed in the late 1960s, was always a bit of a jumble. As Steven Tipton reflected in 1982, "the counterculture itself comprised a wide range of views, some of them at odds with one another."[6] This volume seeks to order, retrospectively, the fragments. I perceive my role in this exercise mainly as that of systematizer and pedant, for the counterculture made its own case quite articulately. The brighter hippies were highly literate in their vitality; the counterethics was important because it offered an innovative appraisal of American culture and promulgated creative, if unorthodox, guidelines for conduct in a rapidly changing society.

There will be no effort made here to reconcile the counterethics with any other system. At some points it obviously overlaps conventional Judaeo-Christian ethical thinking, but to try to say that the counterculture represents mainly a dynamic restatement of the best of that ethical tradition misses the point. Here the counterethics is simply presented on its own terms.

✳ ✳ ✳ What Was the Counterculture?

The counterculture was a romantic social movement of the late 1960s and very early 1970s, mainly composed of teenagers and persons in their early twenties, who through their flamboyant lifestyle expressed their alienation from mainstream American life. *Counterculture,* written as one word or two, became the standard term for the movement (or nonmovement, as some would have it) after the appearance, in 1969, of Theodore Roszak's influential book *The Making of a Counter Culture.*[7] Until then, several competing terms described the cultural revolt of the young; other early contenders were *alternative culture* and *the underground.*

Any culture, of course, can spawn its countercultures, and thus the hippies were part of a long tradition of cultural demurring. In many ways their most obvious and immediate predecessors were the bohemians and beatniks who inhabited earlier decades of the twentieth century. The progression from beat to hip is a fairly obvious one; the beats of the 1950s advocated dropping out of society, promoted new forms of art and literature, smoked marijuana, listened to unorthodox music (jazz), rejected traditional sexual norms, and even popularized the word "hip." One of the first books (1966) to notice the first stirrings of what would become hippie culture in the East Village of New York was plausibly entitled *The New Bohemia.*[8]

Behind both the 1960s counterculture and its predecessor beat culture lay black America. Although the hippies were mainly white (more about that later), they were cultural outsiders, renegades who deviated from the American Way of Life. Black radicals (Malcolm X, W. E. B. duBois) were countercultural heroes because they refused to compromise with the white and prosperous Establishment. Black musicians gave heart as well as soul to hip music. (Bob Dylan and the Beatles may have been the principal cultural icons, but the energy of Chuck Berry and Little Richard wrote the grammar of rock.) Black musicians were smoking marijuana decades before white dropouts had heard of it. Norman Mailer was writing about beatniks in his 1957 essay "The White Negro," but his observations apply equally to hippies:

It is no accident that the source of Hip is the Negro for he has been living on the margin between totalitarianism and democracy for two centuries. But the presence of Hip as a working philosophy in the sub-philosophies of American life is probably due to jazz. . . . In this wedding of the white and the black it was the Negro who brought the cultural dowry. Any Negro who wishes to live must live with danger from his first day.

And, Mailer concluded, even the jargon of hip was shaped in major part by "the Negro jazzman who was the cultural mentor of a people."[9]

The counterculture's participants, usually called hippies, found themselves cast adrift from the prevailing values of society and tried, variously, to effect major changes in majority society or to drop out of it. As the hippies saw things, the Establishment—the tired, entrenched, declining dominant system—was rotten to the core, and a new society needed to arise on the cultural dunghill. Some hippies were escapists who simply favored withdrawal from the prevailing culture; others proposed much more active opposition to and confrontation with it as a necessary step on the road to cultural freedom and progress.

The counterculture had a vocal separatist minority which rejected the dominant culture wholesale and proclaimed the necessity of creating a new, independent, egalitarian society, although the means for getting there were usually murky. Separatist rhetoric could be powerful: one notable separatist document, "The Declaration of Cultural Evolution," written in 1968 by a committee including Timothy Leary, Allen Ginsberg, Paul Krassner, and Abbie Hoffman, listed, in a style imitative of the Declaration of Independence, grievances against majoritarian society—political repression, destruction of the environment, war, and the like. The Declaration maintained that the counterculture had pointed the way to needed social changes, but that "many have been deaf to the voice of reason and consanguinity." Therefore, "human beings everywhere are, and quite properly ought to be, absolved from all allegiance to the present Cultural Arrangements insofar as they are obsolete and harmful."[10]

Similarly another early theoretician of hip, Art Johnston, denounced the "Ethic of the Cool" in the West, which he defined as conformity to the status quo, the only goal of which was getting a good return on one's investment. He wrote that since it was very difficult to live outside the existing system, the function of the counterculture was defiance of the dominant mores. The counterculture was rebellion, a living protest vote, a declaration of choice—the Great Refusal to cooperate.[11]

Still another separatist, Jean-Jacques Lebel, wrote, in terms reminiscent of Herbert Marcuse, of a "containment industry" that aimed to pacify and neutralize the American young. It operated by separating art from life (that is, by having professional artists who displaced popular spontaneous art), by advancing symbolic freedom that did not have a daily-life counterpart (as in nude theatre), and by taking a financial profit from mass-produced imitation hip culture. "This is the 'liberal' version of Hitler's 'final solution' of the youth problem. . . . I say it is time for us to create our own culture, our own lives."[12]

On the whole, however, the counter culture proposed not so much a confrontation with mainstream culture as a simple withdrawal from it. As Lawrence Lipton put it in 1968, "The hippies have passed beyond American society. They're not really living in the same society. . . . It's not so much that they're living on the leftovers, on the waste of American society, as that they just don't give a damn."[13] Or, as Raymond Mungo wrote, "we . . . long ago commenced on our own total Moratorium on constructive participation in this society."[14]

Withdrawal often meant heading for a hip commune. The communes, so the theory went, were not aimed at cultural confrontation, but simply were a turning away to build a new society apart from the old. Down on the commune, a hipster wrote in 1969, "We are in Amerika, but we are no longer a part of it."[15]

From what were the hippies so alienated? Why did they see an alternative, be it confrontive or simply escapist, as necessary? The widespread sense of the counterculture was that it was simply impossible to cope with the dominant American culture any longer. America was a treadmill, a swamp of mediocrity, an emotional pressure cooker; it had become a series of meaningless institutions that transcended persons and developed lives of their own. Moreover, America had become Amerika (the German spelling evoked the Nazis), an oppressor of dissenters. Worse, it was all boring. Widespread mental illness and compulsive violence showed that there was a deep-running malaise in the culture; the rational alternative, as the hippies saw it, was simply to drop out.

But even dropping out was hard to do. Hippie communes were not welcome in many neighborhoods. Rock festivals were banned at every turn. Nonviolent psychedelic chemists ended up in prison. Establishment culture—which was, after all, in the driver's seat—was not willing to tolerate the deviant behavior of the new alternative. As one hippie wrote, "They sense a threat to their continued . . . dominance. And they are absolutely correct."[16]

✳ ✳ ✳ The Generation Gap

Age did not a hippie make or unmake (there were, after all, a few older hippies and lots of young straights), but it is abundantly clear that most counterculturists were relatively young (under thirty, as the catchphrase had it) and that there was great distrust among the hippies of persons very far beyond adolescence. Many writers on both sides of the chasm depicted a "generation gap" that constituted a major battle-line between youth and adults. Theodore Roszak helped promote the concept in *The Making of a Counter Culture*, depicting as critical formative agents Allen Ginsberg's 1950s poem *Howl*, which condemned the parental generation by identifying it with the evil Moloch, and *Mad* magazine, which steadily presented a fairly consistent cynicism about "adult" culture to a very large young audience.[17] Within the counterculture, the generation gap was much discussed. The old was moribund; revolutionary cultural change was imminent. One polemicist, Jack G. Burgess, proclaimed,

[You are standing on a generation that] WILL NOT BE STOOD UPON!

You have declared illegal virtually every establishment, event, gathering, device, and instrument we consider important and worthwhile.

[BUT] YOU CANNOT STOP THE HANDS OF TIME AND YOU CANNOT STILL THE WINDS OF CHANGE!

YOU ARE DYING! Time is removing you from the face of this earth.[18]

In a more analytical frame of mind, underground writer George D. Maloney in 1968 pictured society as broadly divided by age groups into three major generations: under thirty, thirty to forty-five, and over forty-five. The problem of the thirty–to–forty-five generation, he argued, was a simple one: its members were children of the Depression, were unable to shake their preoccupation with security when prosperity returned, and thus were never much concerned with human values. Maloney saw as hopeless the impasse between "young" and "parental" generations, and proclaimed, "'Tis indeed the stuff of which revolutions are made."[19]

The hopelessness of the parental generation was a common theme in the underground, but occasionally a note of a brighter future sounded. Andrew Kopkind, writing in *Rolling Stone* about the 1969 Woodstock festival, saw a phoenix of new culture rising from the ashes of "adult" American life:

> What is not illusionary is the reality of a new culture of opposition. It grows out of the disintegration of the old forms, the vinyl and aerosol institutions that carry all the inane and destructive values of privatism, competition, commercialism, profitability and elitism. . . .
>
> It's not a "youth thing" now but a generational event; chronological age is only the current phase.[20]

✳ ✳ ✳ The Counterculture and the New Left

Although there was a widespread sense of a youth culture of opposition at least by 1967, the alternative culture was never a monolith. Within it were at least two quite different approaches to the social crisis: there was a New Left, an overtly political opposition to the dominant culture; and there was hippiedom, the world of the dropouts and cultural dissenters. Most writers analyzing the sixties have grappled with the problem of showing convergences and divergences between the "Heads" and the "Fists," as Laurence Leamer called them.[21] Paul Goodman distinguished the two related movements in classic religious terms: the distinction involved between inward-oriented hippies and outward-oriented activists was, he said, very close to the age-old question of faith and works.[22] The majority of hippies, while often sympathetic to the New Left, weren't much interested in politics and thus saw the counterculture and New Left as distinct movements, even though the line between them was not always precise. A substantial minority, on the other hand, saw the two groups as more alike than different, because they were both sworn opponents of the established regime; therefore, they were to be considered as fingers on one hand, distinct but sharing a common role. The visionary culture the hippies wanted to establish was based on such political ideologies as peace, racial harmony, and equality; the political crusade of the New Left was deeply romantic, and the great majority of the New Leftists lived the cultural values of the hippies, smoking marijuana, engaging in liberated sex, and often living communally.

Richard Neville created a typology, echoed in less precise terms elsewhere, that is useful here. Under the general heading of "The Movement," he saw three fundamental divisions: the New Left, the Underground (i.e., counterculture), and the "militant poor." The New Left consisted primarily of radical political activists, many of them members of organizations such as Students for a Democratic Society and the Student National Coordinating Committee. The militant poor consisted primarily of ethnic revolutionaries and activists, most notably blacks, Chicanos, and Native Americans. Finally, the Underground included "hippies, beats, mystics, madmen, freaks, yippies, crazies, crackpots, communards and anyone who rejects rigid political ideology ('it's a brain disease'). . . ."[23] The New Left and the counterculture both manifested a sharp discontent with American society and its decadent hypocrisy,[24] but they were nonetheless distinct groups.

Some hip writers minimized the differences between the two factions. As P. G. Stafford put it, "The new leftist and the acid head are in fundamental agreement at their political core. At the very least, their experience and thinking puts them both at odds with the man from the right. . . ."[25] Similarly Stan Iverson wrote, "The hippie life style has superficially influenced a broad spectrum of the United States, and is such an influence in the New Left that it is impossible—and I think undesirable—to draw a sharp line of division between the two movements."[26] Ed Sanders, hip author and musician, observed, "We have a commonality of radicalism, smut, chromosome damage, marijuana, street fucking—we know each other."[27] Theodore Roszak also saw a basic oneness beneath the apparent differences: "We grasp the underlying unity of the counter cultural variety, then, if we see beat-hip bohemianism as an effort to work out the personality structure and total life style that follow from New Left social criticism."[28] On one basic point the two schools were in harmony: something is badly wrong with American society, and you, each individual, can do something about it.

Despite the hippies' indifference or hostility toward politics, some observers argued that the counterculture actually had a more substantial political impact on American life than the New Left did, because political action among the hippies emerged from moments of real-life need and because the hippies saw the roots of modern social problems, not merely their symptoms. Paul Goodman noted that hippies "become political when they are indignant . . . and they also have to work at power and politics in order to protect their business and community, e.g. against police harassment; but otherwise they rightly judge that radicals are in a bag."[29]

And whatever the normal distance between the two groups, they did work together on some important occasions. For example, at the October 1967 march on the Pentagon in protest of American involvement in Vietnam, there was a wide range of persons present.[30] Some wanted confrontation, but many merely wanted to form a human circle around the Pentagon in an attempt to levitate it! They worked together—at least for an afternoon—in rare harmony.

The counterculture faulted the New Left at several specific points. A common theme was simply suspicion of organized groups in general: "Mass movements make no sense to me, and I want no part of mass movements. I think this is the error that the leftist activists are making. I see them as young men with menopausal minds."[31]

Others complained that the New Left's absolutist devotion to revolutionary activity deprived it of a humanitarian vision. "When you pick up a gun and learn to kill," wrote Mick Wheelock, "the part of you that loved flowers and simple things will die!"[32] "'Some people will do worse things than any cop, and do them in the name of revolution,' Eldridge Cleaver once told me," noted Raymond Mungo.[33] Ralph J. Gleason, an elder theorist of hip and *Rolling Stone* columnist, summarized the argument:

> The political radicals have the right enemies, they have courage, some of them, they even have a kind of program for Improvement of the Society which makes a kind of sense.
>
> But they all have the old approach. You can't make an omelet

without breaking eggs. True, man, true. But you better figure out how to make a revolution without killing people or it won't work. We've had all that. We really have.[34]

Some faulted the New Left precisely because it embraced logic and ideology; the counterculture, in varying degrees, tended to be suspicious of both. Raymond Mungo exclaimed, "There are no answers! There are no systems! This is not my salvation! Leave me alone!"[35] Similarly Bob Maurice, the producer of the film *Woodstock*, contended that "contemporary radical politics is purely Christian. It's one of the manifestations of Western Christianity. And it's that dichotomy of good versus evil, essentially a Christian one, and it's idealistic. . . . [But] people are too complicated for that."[36]

Some countercultural purists protested that the New Left exploited the counterculture. "David Super-Straight" of the Berkeley *Barb*, for example, blamed the New Left for the decline of the spirit of love, for the rise of harmful drugs (as opposed to sweet dope), for the advent of guns. In particular, he accused the "Ginks of Berkeley" of having tried to organize the early hippies for their own ends, of contriving confrontations between hippies and police in the hope of politicizing the hippies, all because the Ginks wanted power for the sake of power.[37] Mungo noted that the counterculture was especially vulnerable to this sort of exploitation, and that, as a result, hip culture was damaged. To Mungo, political militancy was a "character disorder."[38]

Finally, the counterculture accused the New Left of losing sight of pleasure. Writing of the Woodstock festival, Greil Marcus maintained that the pleasure of dope and casual sex were and should have been undertaken because they were fun, "not because such acts represented scoring points against parents or Richard Nixon or the Reader's Digest."[39] Another person remarked simply, "The New Left writes so many position papers that they have no time for sex. They just take a position."[40]

So the hippie counterculture and the New Left pitched their tents in distinct but adjacent campsites. The two movements could never be truly separate, if only because just behind the flash and color and irreverence of the hippies the grim reaper stood grinning: just over one's shoulder were an ugly war in Asia, a military draft, racism, and impending environmental doom.

If the hippies frequently criticized the New Left, so did the politicals criticize the culturals, and they had sufficient exposure in the underground press to voice their sentiments. Generally, the complaints centered on opposition to dropping out when there was so much revolutionary work to be done and to using dope and drugs—both because they sapped one's revolutionary energies and because they presented the possibility of being arrested for the wrong reason. The New Left castigated the apolitical hippies with invectives like these:

> The psychedelic revolution is not a revolution in any sense of the word. It is a means of escaping the restlessness imposed by everyday life upon everyone in this society. But it is sterile and infantile because it does not fundamentally transform these restrictions which afflict and affect every one of us. . . .
>
> The philosophy of the "hippies" is a philosophy of politics that says there should be love toward everyone. Love is a good thing, but hatred of what is hateful is as necessary and important.[41]

> The immediate Movement reaction to drugs and dropping out was to describe it as playing into the hands of the government, allowing the creation of a totalitarian system whereby the rulers provided free drugs for the people (or at least the dissenters) in order to keep them happily and quietly oppressed. LSD was bread and circuses, the ultimate pacification program.[42]

The differences between counterculture and New Left sometimes aroused hostility on both sides. David McReynolds wrote in 1967 of a meeting to plan an antiwar rally, at which Richard Alpert (later known as Ram Dass) delivered a long diatribe urging people to boycott the planned rally because some people there would burn their draft cards, and it would be "bad public relations for the psychedelic community to be involved in that kind of thing." McReynolds, writing up the incident, blasted Alpert: "I do not mock the man who seeks out the God within him. But I do mock the man who, in one breath, tells every youth to follow his own light and in the next breath warns him about public relations."[43]

Such was the typical New Leftist attitude toward the counterculture. But there was also a periodic recognition, in some leftist circles, that the hippies made an important contribution to radical politics just by their existence. No less a leftist than Herbert Marcuse called the hippies "the only viable social revolution" of the day, arguing that despite their disinterest in Marxism, they were having a revolutionary impact because they opposed a repressive social system, "reject[ed] the junk they're supposed to buy now, . . . reject[ed] the war . . . reject[ed] the competitive performances."[44]

A generation later, Marcuse's observations still hold up. As Andrew Kimbrell argued in 1988, the New Left's agenda was actually not a fundamental threat to society: civil rights of blacks, women, and others could be ensured by law, the war could be ended, the environment could be protected—all without making major inroads on the basic structure of society. After all, the New Left did not challenge the supremacy of reason, the notion that material prosperity is the supreme goal of society, the sanctity of economic growth, or the belief that spiritual values constituted an opiate, or at least were unimportant. By contrast, the counterculture

> though often acting in a drugged haze, attacked society at a more fundamental level than the New Left. Through experiments with lifestyles and philosophies, it challenged, if only by implication, the assumptions of most Americans about politics, knowledge, materialism, technology, and what constitutes the "good life."[45]

✳ ✳ ✳ Race, Class, and Gender in a Largely White, Male-Defined Movement

The hippies were mainly children of privilege, and their outlook reflected their heritage. They glorified poverty and sometimes lived in it; they championed the rights of racial minorities and, to some extent, women. But the movement came from a prosperous, white, male-defined segment of society. Perhaps it was inevitable that those who would reject middle-class comforts had to come from comfortable backgrounds; the have-nots of society had no material luxuries to rebel against.

Black hippies were unusual. They did show up occasionally, and they were readily accepted by the white majority. Their numbers, however, were never large. Blacks interested in dissent from the prevailing culture tended to be more interested in racial-political than flower-child activities. It is noteworthy, though, that militant blacks, while critical of all who would not join the revolutionary struggle, regarded the hippies as allies, not enemies. In 1968, an editorial in the *Black Panther*, the most widely read militant black publication, defined the Black Panther Party's position in its usual mince-no-words style:

> Black brothers stop vamping on the hippies. They are not your enemy. Your enemy, right now, is the white racist pigs who support this corrupt system. . . . Your enemy is not the hippies. . . . WE HAVE NO QUARREL WITH THE HIPPIES. LEAVE THEM ALONE. Or the BLACK PANTHER PARTY will deal with you![46]

Certainly the counterculture was male-defined. As the following chapters will suggest, authorship in the underground press was overwhelmingly male. Women were commonly "chicks"; when they were in relationships with men, they were "old ladies." It is important to remember, however, that the heyday of the counterculture, which was in the late 1960s, came along before the prominent advent of the contemporary feminist movement, which began to attract serious, widespread attention only about 1968 or 1969, just as the counterculture was starting to wind down. At least at first, the male hippies were as disinclined as males elsewhere in society to allow women equal rights and privileges; the gap between egalitarian hippie rhetoric and male hippie actions may have had some influence on the emerging feminists, many of whom had deep roots in the counterculture. If the writers quoted in subsequent chapters tend to be male, and if hippie ideas seem largely male-defined, it is because that was the dominant orientation of the hippies in their prime years.

✳ ✳ ✳ The Counterculture and American Religion

Many ethical systems are theological or religious in basis; if the hippies had an ethic, one may naturally ask whether or not they constituted a religious movement. The answer hinges mainly on how one defines *religion*. Definitions that involve institutions and rituals supporting a clearly articulated religious quest would leave the hippies out; most counterculturists did not see hipness as religious per se, even if there were religious movements (such as the dope churches and various Eastern movements) within the hip world. Definitions that involve such concepts as ultimate concern, however, could well include the hippies. The counterculture was a movement of seekers of meaning and value, a movement which thus embodied the historic quest of any religion. Like many dissenting religions, the hippies were enormously hostile to the religious institutions of the dominant culture, and they tried to find new and adequate ways to do the tasks the dominant religions failed to perform.

Some outside observers regarded the hippies as religionists, whether the hippies liked the label or not. Harvey Cox, for example, wrote, shortly after the Summer of Love (1967), that the hippies reminded him of St. Francis:

> Hippieness represents a secular version of the historic American quest for a faith that warms the heart, a religion one can experience deeply and feel intensely. The love-ins are our 20th Century equivalent of the 19th Century Methodist camp meetings—with the same kind of fervor and the same thirst for a God who speaks through emotion and not through anagrams of doctrine. Of course, the Gospel that is preached differs somewhat in content, but then, content was never that important for the revivalist—it was the spirit that counted.
>
> Hippieness has all the marks of a new religious movement. It has its evangelists, its sacred grottoes, its exuberant converts.[47]

Similarly, religion scholar William C. Shepherd found that countercultural religiousness was patent:

> Since a set of symbols, certain ritual practices, and the production of social cohesion are all marks of religious systems, it is fair to say that our counter cultural young have developed a genuine form of religiosity, indeed a quite new form for the West because it does not include doctrines or truth claims about supersensual entities.[48]

Many within the counterculture itself also saw the movement as essentially a new religion, one which drew from many traditions, including Asian and Native American religions as well as Western Christianity and Judaism. West Coast sexual and psychedelic activist Jefferson Poland wrote, "we find ourselves (to our surprise) in a religious revival. Simple atheism is not enough."[49] Ralph J. Gleason, the senior sage of hip, believed that religiosity could not be ignored here or anywhere: "The need to believe is there. The knowledge is implicit in life itself and the desire to believe is so overwhelming that non-belief cannot be tolerated. It is part of the life support system and it must be there."[50]

No sense of religious purpose among the hippies meant, however, that the counterculture had any fondness for the dominant religions of America. To the hippies, the churches and synagogues were mainly hoary vehicles of Establishment thought and activity in its worst form. As one hip writer (rather awkwardly) summarized the critique,

> The churches are as flagrant violators of the natural, real religious way, the way of man in harmony with earth, water, sky and fire, and, of course, his fellows as any other institution. These supposed houses of worship, where one would hope, there might exist something analogous to an institutionalized conscience, are in fact just further examples of sham and hypocrisy. Rather than insist Christians as Christians in the barest sense the word conveys, refrain from supporting the golden calves our government spawns, its campaigns, its waste, its wars, the church instead functions as a Sunday salve . . . assuaging the blunted senses of each cowardly congregation . . . dressed its best for one more Sunday obligation.[51]

Self-righteous centers of hypocrisy, stations for the blessing of the Establishment, wealthy organizations mainly interested in preserving themselves, havens for the narrow-minded, anachronisms utterly irrelevant to modern life—thus were the dominant religions regarded by counterculturists. The whole point of the hip rebellion was to announce the New, and the prevailing religious institutions stood foursquare for the Old. They were part of the problem, not part of the solution.

There were exceptions, of course. There were radicals here and there in the mainline religions; the hippies saw the radical Catholic priests Dan and Phil Berrigan, for example, as "righteous Christians."[52] Indeed, some hippies perceived that the Establishment religions were rooted in radicalism, even though they had lost their radical perspective over history.[53] But the dissenters were not in charge in the dominant religious bodies, and radical roots were of limited value when the tree had withered.

A few saw the counterculture as a purifying element for decadent religious bodies, a revival movement that just might help restore right thinking to lost churches. As a hip couple wrote in Berkeley, "The young people we meet in the LSD underground appear to be groping toward . . . a renewal of religion, a Religion of Loving, Dancing, and Much Music. Making 'A Joyful Noise Unto the Lord!'—a personal as well as group unifying religion . . . based on 'The Unmediated Vision.' "[54]

In any event, there were divisions so profound between the hippies and the prevailing religions that expecting the hippies to have much influence on the big religions was simply unrealistic. Most hippies believed that certain drugs provided one acceptable way to try to approach the mysteries of the universe. The hippies were vocal proponents of liberated sexuality, whereas the dominant religions were society's main bastions of restricted sex. Even the most religious of the hippies tended to take unusual (by traditional American standards) approaches to religion, often emphasizing Eastern spiritual teachings, and they were often syncretistic, pursuing a sort of religiosity that combined elements ranging from Hindu mysticism to Neopaganism to Ouija boards. It's a fair guess that most hippies would not have been very welcome in most churches; for their part, the hippies were not interested in getting active in any conventional religious body.

✳ ✳ ✳ Resource Materials

The counterculture was so productive of literary materials that any research, even in this cybernetic age, must necessarily be selective in regard to its source materials. The basic body of materials that I have used has been the underground newspapers. Certainly the underground press is not the only source of data on the counterculture, nor is it necessarily the best. It was, however, the most distinctive literary creation of the counterculture and received extremely wide acceptance in the world of hip, along with attention, if not acclaim, elsewhere.[55] It also gives the researcher fairly stable materials with which to deal—much more reflective of the period than interviews, for example, would be. Literary materials composed by and for the counterculture may be seen in their original form by any outside observer; interviews conducted decades later could hardly be as honestly representative of the spirit of the age, however much nuance and anecdote they might produce.

The underground press is also a valuable source in that it actually employed two media, words and visual art. The counterculture was a highly visual phenomenon, what with gaudy clothing, psychedelic posters, decorated cars and vans, and the like. The underground press was full of the distinctive and striking art of the counterculture and thus helps to convey more fully than most other materials a sense of the integration of sensory experience which the counterculture strove for. Art was understood to be one of the fronts of the multifaceted cultural revolution, and the underground press was loaded with it.

It should be emphasized that the underground papers were primary countercultural documents. They were written, edited, pasted up, and published by hippies. The underground papers were usually small, usually nonpaying, usually hand-to-mouth operations. They were papers of passion, not detachment. Thus there is no need here to try to account for the bias of reporters; they were enthusiastic participants in the culture they were covering. Collectively, the underground papers contain, I would argue, the clearest extended statement counterculturists ever made of their ideals and values.

Thus this book uses the underground press as its primary resource, because no better body of material for studying hippie culture exists. At least three substantial microfilmed collections of underground newspapers have been compiled;[56] the Bell and Howell collection, comprising 67 rolls of microfilm, has excellent breadth of coverage and has provided runs of most of the papers used in this study. The collection covers the years 1965 to 1970, which amply embrace the rise and flowering of the counterculture. (Abe Peck, in his definitive history of the underground press in both its cultural and political phases, defines his temporal turf as 1964 through 1973, but most of the material important to my study was published by 1970.[57]) The Bell and Howell collection contains about five hundred individual periodical titles; in order to make this project manageable I limited my research to sixty-five representative and significant titles, all from the United States. Attention was paid to selecting papers from the East and West Coasts, especially from New York and the San Francisco Bay area, the two most important urban centers of countercultural activity, although care was also taken to sample papers from all parts of the country. Papers often cited by underground writers as influential were included. Papers used were those with a generally cultural focus; those with a primarily political focus (such as some of the New Left publications, including *New Left Notes*) were omitted from the sample, as were papers with other special interests and constituencies (*Faculty Peace News*, *Black Panther*, *Free Palestine*). I read the complete run of each of the sixty-five papers as contained in the Bell and Howell collection plus any other copies of those papers I could obtain separately.

For perspective, use has also been made of a few other miscellaneous underground papers (including some from the generally excluded categories above), of other hip writings (especially books written for the hip audience), and of writings of sympathetic observers (Theodore Roszak and Paul Goodman are archetypes here). Academic scholars and other outside observers of the hippies have been cited as well, but use of their material has been sparing. The point of this volume is to present the distinctive ethics of the hippies on the hippies' own terms, from primary materials.

Writers for the underground papers were mostly male; thus this study is not perfectly representative of hippiedom, just as the underground papers are not. Also, the papers tended to lionize and publish the writings of certain countercultural celebrities. Works by and about Timothy Leary and Allen Ginsberg, to name perhaps the two most prominent examples, were published very frequently. Thus there may be an elitist tilt to this study, just as there was to the underground press.

The underground papers have been cited by date where possible. Where dates have been illegible or missing, citations have been made by volume and issue number. Obvious typographical errors have been corrected, but otherwise the material has not been altered; thus errors of usage and fact have not been corrected in quotations.

CHAPTER 2

The Ethics of Dope

Pursuing the religious life today without using psychedelic drugs is like studying

astronomy with the naked eye because that's how they did it in the first

century A.D., and besides, telescopes are unnatural.

—Timothy Leary, *The Politics of Ecstasy*, 1968

Smoke dope everywhere. . . . Dope is Great, it's fun, it's healthy. . . . Get every

creature so stoned they can't stand the plastic shit of American culture. . . . Smoke

dope, it's your duty to future generations, turn the world on, it's your duty to the

universe.

—"Pun," *Other Scenes*, June 1968

Nothing else was so characteristic of the counterculture as dope. The overwhelming majority of hippies used it, and the few who didn't approved of its use by others. The commitment to—as opposed to furtive use of—dope was the single largest symbol of the difference between counterculture and Establishment culture.

The use of the term *dope* here instead of *drugs* is deliberate. To the hippies, it served to draw a line between the drugs perceived to be good and those deemed bad. Dope was good; drugs, on the other hand, included both good and bad substances. The distinction was imprecise, of course; hippies disagreed a great deal about where the line between good and bad should be drawn. Very generally, most hippies approved of such substances as marijuana, hashish, LSD, psilocybin, mescaline, peyote, and morning glory seeds; they were less approving, and often outspokenly critical, of amphetamines, methadrine, DMT, STP, barbiturates, the opiates, and sometimes cocaine. Psychedelics were good; speed and downers were bad. Substances that were perceived as expanding consciousness were good; things that made the user dumb were bad. But each individual made his or her own choices. There was no universally accepted dividing line between the two categories.

Tom Coffin was one hip writer who delineated the distinction between dope and drugs:

> We're talking about and doing Revolution, attack on all fronts, political, educational, religious, cultural, even *business*. . . . And dope is part of that revolution, and if you fear dope (Dope, not DRUGS—alcohol is a drug, pot is DOPE; nicotine is a DRUG, acid is DOPE; DRUGS turn you off, dull your senses, give you the strength to face another day in Death America, DOPE turns you on, heightens sensory awareness, sometimes twists them out of shape and you experience that too, gives you vision and clarity, necessary to create Life from Death) if you fear DOPE more than you fear Richard Nixon and his Machined Men of Death, then you have indeed sold out and bought in. . . . The difference between Stupor and Ecstasy is the difference between Jack Daniels and Orange Sunshine, between the Pentagon and Woodstock, between *The New York Times* and *Good Times*. We all have to make our choices.[1]

Usage in this chapter will follow this popular hippie perspective; *dope* will be good and *drugs* bad, except that in some cases *drugs* will be inclusive of both types. I avoid those terms only in quotations, where the author's language will stand.

Virtually everyone in the counterculture agreed that dope, whatever its correct name, was great. One all-star symposium sponsored by LEMAR International (the marijuana-legalization lobby), whose participants included Timothy Leary, Allen Ginsberg, Leslie Fiedler, Abbie Hoffman, and Jerry Rubin, "agreed that the biggest problem with drugs is shitty drug laws and the bad research."[2] The counterculture saw the main "drug problems" as spotty quality and high prices.

Dope was utterly intrinsic to the counterculture. The hippies believed that dope itself had altered the consciousness of millions of individuals in fundamental ways, and that that alteration was inevitably a major force in the establishment of the new culture. So contended Richard Alpert (later Ram Dass) when he wrote, "We've moved in the direction of a whole new model of the human brain. . . . You can travel anywhere, back into childhood, back through evolutionary history, cosmic history, down your own bloodstream or nervous system."[3] And it made the new culture sweet. As Jan Hodenfield wrote about the Woodstock festival, "Equal to the outside's anger and concern about the 'drug menace' was its awe at the 'politeness,' the 'good behavior,' the 'cheer-fulness,' the 'lack of violence.' And the two were never connected." [4]

Dope, though good, was never seen as problem-free. What was important was that the downside was dwarfed by the upside. As Raymond Mungo wrote, ". . . for us, everything is possible; if the heart is willing, what ecstatic adventure is too risky? *What is risk?*" [5]

So dope was a constitutive element of the counterculture. As Leary put it, "You have to learn the outside dope which is TV, and the inside dope which are drugs, and if you don't someone's going to do it for you and they're going to cop your mind completely. That's why your only hope is dope." [6]

From the perspective of a quarter-century later, it is easy to observe that the hippies were overly optimistic about the power dope held for good and naive about the downside of drugs in general. However, the hippies enunciated an ethic of drugs that made more overall sense than any ethics or policies prevailing in the drug-hysterical 1990s. The main elements of the hip ethics of dope looked something like this: Use it positively. Use it sanely. Know what you're doing. Avoid bad drugs. Avoid misuse of (good) dope. Don't use dope to hurt others. Assert your freedom to make your own decisions about dope. And have a good trip.

✳ ✳ ✳ The Spread of Dope

A UCLA professor was quoted in the days of hip as saying that "if a young man hasn't smoked pot by the time he's twenty, he's probably sick," that is, "seriously neurotic," because marijuana is "a way of life for America's youth." [7] Evidence from the hip era suggests that indeed huge numbers of the young were smoking it. A sample of 219 University of Kansas students in 1971 indicated that 69 percent had smoked marijuana and that 92 percent had friends who smoked it. [8] A 1971 Gallup Poll reportedly found that over 40 percent of college students had tried pot, a percentage "eight times as high as [that] recorded in a 1967 survey." [9] The College Poll found that in 1972, 60 percent of college students had used marijuana and noted that "the results of this annual drug study belie the theory that drug use on the campus is abating. It was generally thought that the drug culture was a unique one which would generally lose favor as the troubled era of the late 60s and early 1970s passed away. This now appears to be false." [10]

The National Commission on Marihuana and Drug Abuse, in its extensive survey published in 1972, found that twenty-four million Americans had smoked marijuana; the incidence of use reached 40 percent in the eighteen-to-twenty-one age group, and 38 percent in the twenty-two-to-twenty-five age group. [11] Lewis Yablonsky, in a study that specifically focused on the counterculture in 1968, found that 90.7 percent of his sample had used marijuana and that 68.2 percent had used LSD. [12] All in all, dope achieved widespread use among youth in general and it was the common denominator of the counterculture.

Massive increases in arrests and border seizures accompanied the spread of dope. [13] But neither stemmed the tide of dope. The New York *Times* estimated that 99 percent of the crowd at Woodstock were smoking marijuana, and a state police sergeant was quoted as commenting, "As far as I know, the narcotics guys are not arresting anybody for grass. If we did, there wouldn't be enough space in Sullivan County, or the next three counties, to put them in." [14] Many hippies believed that they were looking the future directly in the eye: "The drug revolution is with us, despite border shutdowns, surveillance techniques, police, everything. It's a revolution that's sweeping the world." [15]

Even before Woodstock, as early as 1967, hundreds could gather for smoke-ins without fear of arrest. Marijuana's sweet smoke permeated society; even Kim Agnew, the daughter of the staunchly antidope vice-president Spiro Agnew, was busted in 1969. [16]

Something was happening, Mr. Jones. The psychoactive properties of marijuana had been known in the United States since the turn of the century, but the use of grass had spread only very slowly until the 1960s. [17] LSD and its unusual effects were discovered in 1938, but the chemical was hardly used until the middle 1960s, at which time it was still being sold legally. [18] With the emergence of the counterculture, however, marijuana quickly spread to the point that hippies could boast that it was "so widely used, it's unofficially legal." [19] And LSD wasn't far behind.

* * * Why Hippies (and Other People) Did Dope

Hip theoreticians had many explanations for the great surge of dope use. Three general schools of thought dominated the multifaceted debate: dope is fun; dope is revolutionary; and dope is good for body and soul.

Certainly fun was a part of it. The counterculture was deliberately hedonistic; the hippie creed was "If it feels good, then do it so long as it doesn't hurt anyone else."[20] Hippies were perhaps the first to detect a social anomaly, that American society had seen an exponential growth in leisure, yet was still suspicious of fun for its own sake. A seventy-five-year-old hippie (!) commented upon being arrested:

> In our culture it's wrong to do anything for pleasure. You have to have a higher motive. Well, I take it just because I like it. That's the only reason I would do anything. I don't do a thing under compulsion. And there's no reason to be ashamed of something I like. I say, God dammit, when I sleep with a woman or take a drink I'm not doing it for anybody. If I do it I do it for myself. So why not with everything else?[21]

Yet there was usually a streak of rebellion in the pleasure ethic. The fact that fun was suspect was a reminder, the hippies argued, that Americans lived in cultural confinement and that the time had come for a social revolution. Dope was revolutionary because the larger society, which had learned to tolerate some types of deviant behavior, was utterly flabbergasted by this new challenge. Very quickly the use of dope became a cultural symbol, a means of thumbing one's nose at society. One counterculturist wrote, "People are taking drugs in repudiation of something—something most young people can see and understand, although we sometimes have a hard time defining it."[22] As a West Coast hip author concluded in 1969, "The government is right in its stand on drugs. They are a definite threat to society. . . . Drugs . . . must be ruthlessly suppressed lest the people feel too good."[23]

On the other hand, fun and rebellion were hardly the whole story. For many some of the time, and for some all of the time, dope was a tool that provided healing and insight. More than a few hippies claimed to have found through dope startling new insights and sometimes a comprehensive philosophy of life. As one wrote, drugs could be related to the search for authentic human existence where a person is not alienated from himself and estranged from his fellow man and where God is more than a dead word. It is just possible that the drug scene is more closely tied to the province of existential questions of philosophy and theology than those of law or even medicine.[24]

Furthermore, American society demanded the spiritual search which dope seemed to make simple. Sensitive persons, counterculturists argued, had real trouble coexisting with the jive crap of American life—the race for money and status, the dehumanization that pervaded technological society. Dopers thus were Luddites who symbolically smashed the machines with their substances. A humanized society might not have required a chemical escape hatch; as hip author Tom Coffin put it, "Were the real problems, of war and racism, alienation and anomie, poverty and pollution, to be solved (or even honestly worked on), the culturally-induced need for consciousness expanding drugs would be perhaps nil."[25] That was the point of Timothy Leary's frequent assertion that "Your only hope is dope." Leary's associate, Richard Alpert, before he became Baba Ram Dass, similarly intoned, "We are not junkies, not in it just for kicks, nor are we sick. There is no category for us."[26]

✳ ✳ ✳ Legalization

Although some theorists of hip argued seriously that dope needed to be illegal to maintain its revolutionary qualities, the vast majority, logically enough, supported legalization. As one wrote, "The issue isn't after all whether pot smoking is good or bad for us. The issue is how much longer and to what extent we can allow the state to control our minds."[27] Psychedelic guru Art Kleps agreed: "Your body is your own. If you don't own your own body, if you can't do what you wish with your own body short of hurting somebody else, then you're no better than a domestic animal."[28] In a similar vein, Stephen Gaskin, the leader of The Farm, one of the most prominent hip communes, promulgated this manifesto: "We believe that if a vegetable and an animal want to get together and can be heavier together than either one of them alone, it shouldn't be anybody else's business."[29] So basic was the issue that Allen Ginsberg once demanded a Congressional investigation find out just who was responsible for this "vast swindle" of illegal dope.[30] Wasn't freedom, after all, a paramount American value?

But there were always a few working the other side of the street. Some quite seriously believed that dope's value as a tool for challenging prevailing social values would be lost with legalization. Others argued that legalized dope would provide a windfall for capitalists, that an impersonal commercial dope industry would grow up, complete with advertising and high prices, and that such an industry would contradict the very essence of dope. Some simply argued that campaigning for what should be automatic was degrading: "Free men do not ask permission to enjoy their freedom."[31]

Some contended that dope should be legalized because it provided profound insights; others made a straightforward civil-libertarian case for legalization. Still others, though, simply noted that the great increase in the use of dope, which stemmed from the hippies' popularization of it, made continued prohibition impractical. Comparisons were often made with failed prohibitions of the past, especially the classic American experiment with the prohibition of alcohol. Howard Moody in 1972 listed several failed prohibitions: coffee drinking in the Near East in the seventeenth century; tobacco in sixteenth- and seventeenth-century Europe; marijuana in North Africa in the late 1950s; and the American prohibition of alcohol. Despite draconian penalties—capital punishment, in some cases—those efforts all failed.[32] So why not bite the legalization bullet?

✳ ✳ ✳ The Dope Churches

The dope churches were a marvelously variegated counter-cultural phenomenon. Some evoked deep mystical religious experiences; others simply amounted to attempts to get around the drug laws. Some were deadly serious; some were whimsically lighthearted. Collectively they were one of the quainter byways of hip.[33]

The Native American Church, which predated the hippies by roughly half a century, was much admired by the hip-era dope churches. The Native American Church not only had a historic tradition of drug use for ritual purposes, it was the only place where a psychedelic drug, peyote, could be used legally. Many hippies were infatuated with Native American culture anyway. So the Native American Church was an object of fascination for serious dopers. But since the church was generally open only to ethnic American Indians, the hippies were left to devise their own imitations of it.

No hip dope church, however, really resembled the Native American Church very much. For American Indians, the Native American Church was and is not primarily focused on getting high. Rather it is a way of getting in touch with ancient native traditions, of calling up through intricate and timeless rituals the wisdom of millennia of tribal culture. Peyote has always been one of several spiritual tools; its use has been guided and controlled by elders whose spiritual experience has made them leaders. Hippies wanted to get high, and perhaps to see any vision that might be conjured up thereby; Native American Church members wanted to preserve and revive ancient traditions, including the visionary experience. Despite the large differences between hippies and Native Americans, however, the hippies genuinely admired and often imitated Indian ways; and at least some Indians felt affinity for the young dissenters who voluntarily placed themselves outside the oppressive social mainstream.

Within the counterculture the most "serious" dope church, in religious terms, was Tim Leary's League for Spiritual Discovery. Leary wanted to avoid any organization at all for his psychedelic spirituality, keeping his religion "pure" and aloof from social structures. However, any use of dope meant challenging or evading the law, so Leary organized the League as an advocacy agency for chemical freedom.[34] As he described it, "We're not a religion in the sense of the Methodist Church seeking new adherents. We're a religion in the basic primeval sense of a tribe living together and centered around shared spiritual goals."[35] "In our religion the temple is the human body, the shrine is the home, and the congregation is a small group of family members and friends."[36] The actual content of Leary's, and presumably therefore the League's, religion resembled some Hindu traditions, but the real point of having an organization was to push for the legalization of dope for sacramental, or at least spiritual, purposes. With the League came Leary's "Two Commandments for the Molecular Age": (1) Thou Shalt Not Alter the Consciousness of thy fellow man. (2) Thou Shalt Not Prevent thy fellow man from Altering his own Consciousness.[37] Leary described the League as "dedicated to the ancient sacred sequence of turning-on, tuning-in and dropping-out. Its aim is to help create every man as God and every woman as Goddess."[38]

> We're saying the same thing Luther said to Rome: take the Bible and stand naked in your communication with God. Now the particular method we use is artificial. It shocked Rome when Luther said he could take this man-made thing and find God through it. He didn't need the apparatus of this enormous Church. It shocks Americans today when we say that anyone in a state of grace can take this chemical and stand naked before this Divine Process.[39]

Another psychedelic church of the personality-cult variety was the Neo-American Church, headed by Chief Boo-Hoo (the name is deliberately silly; one shouldn't take oneself too seriously) Art Kleps. Kleps and Leary were friends and at one time mutual admirers, but their churches were largely dissimilar. Kleps explained the difference thus: "Leary has a religion; he is a spiritual leader. I am functioning like a pope who is nothing more than a super-business man."[40] Satire was the centerpiece of Neo-Americanism, which contended that "The United States Government and all other churches are shared fantasies. . . ."[41] Was its chief attraction the possibility that sometime its members just might get legalized dope? "Yeah," answered Kleps, "I think that has a lot to do with it. And why not? The Catholic Church certainly doesn't hesitate to use all kinds of arguments of the same kind to seduce people into joining."[42] The Neo-American Church had religiosity mixed with cynicism, satire, and lack of respect for propriety, all of which renders the group hard to characterize easily. And characterization is more difficult than ever once the inquirer has read the group's special scripture, *The Boo-Hoo Bible*,[43] certainly a product of nonlinear thinking.

A much more "serious" organization, and one that stood essentially apart from the counterculture, was the Church of the Awakening. Founded in 1963 by John Aiken, a retired physician, it advocated the use of dope "as an aid to meditation," and thus was interested in the legalization of dope, but at the same time tried to keep a middle-class orientation. If Kleps represented the left wing of psychedelic religion, the Church of the Awakening represented the right. Its religious concern was entirely serious; as Aiken said, implicitly disparaging other dope churches, "We're not there just to promote the use of psychedelics."[44]

Beyond these four prominent groups there were several other psychedelic churches, most of which seem to have been short-lived. Among them were the Shiva Fellowship Church, the Psychedelic Venus Church, the Fellowship of the Clear Light, the American Council of Internal Divinity, and the Psychedelic Peace Fellowship.[45] They ranged from relatively conservative (along the lines of the Church of the Awakening) to absurd (some groups appear to have been more whimsical than religious), but all shared a basic desire to legitimize the psychedelic religious experience.

Beneath the dope churches lay serious concern for the right of individuals to use dope, especially for religious purposes, without interference from any outside source. All professed a libertarian attitude toward dope, and all argued that dope was more than just fun, that it was a true sacrament.

Few hippies argued that dope *couldn't* be used as a sacrament, but some were nevertheless skeptical of psychedelic religiosity. Some politicos complained that heavily religious use of dope led to the pursuit of spiritual experience at the expense of social concern. A more common complaint was that the religionists were sometimes narrow in that they tended to restrict dope to the religious sphere and deny its secular usefulness as fun or escapism.[46] However, the critics generally agreed that dope churches pointed up a legitimate concern for internal freedom and thus were a valuable part of the counterculture.

✳ ✳ ✳ The Ethical Case for Dope

Hippies didn't just tolerate dope; they said people *should* use it. Counterculturists argued that dope was distinctly useful to just about anyone in several specific ways.

Dope as a Means of Understanding and Coping with the Evils of American Culture. As symptom, dope reflected dissatisfaction with the prevailing culture. But the hippies saw it as an agent as well as a symptom.

Dope, it was argued, could enhance that dissatisfaction by clarifying one's understanding of the great errors of Establishment society. As some hippies put it, dope made people understand the cultural disease on the cellular, as opposed to the intellectual, level; the individual then had to choose between dropping out of that culture as nearly as possible and trying to remain within it, but with a perspective that made it bearable, a perspective involving a certain detachment that said that life could be lived fully even within a generally meaningless culture—with, of course, the help of insights gained with the aid of dope. An anonymous hippie wrote in 1970, "If nothing else can be said for marijuana, it can be praised as a cultural detoxicant; it acts as an emotional detergent that breaks through the sham and hypocrisy and living-death of much of contemporary America, and allows that vision of beauty that American life seems so bent on destroying."[47]

Ram Dass (then Richard Alpert) once said that the role of dope was "quite simply to upset the apple cart."[48] And there was value in that upset: "Drugs break patterns, that's all they do. When patterns are broken, new worlds can emerge."[49] With the psychedelics, value systems changed; people became more aware than before of their social conditioning and more interested in overcoming that conditioning to live lives based on choice rather than inevitability.

Some key insights were said to come while one was high, but they carried over to life in general, and thus dope was critical because it was held to form the basis of an entirely new way of thinking. Moreover, it was widely believed that once a person came to this new way of thinking, and consequently living, he or she would have trouble reverting to former patterns. Dope, the hippies argued, engendered a profound revolution in consciousness. Most counterculturists agreed with Will Albert that this revolution would have an "ultimately beneficial effect on our society."[50] It showed the way out of the rat race to a more comfortable, relaxing, and meaningful way of life.

Dope and Religious Experience. So many hippies believed dope was in some way productive of religious experience[51] that a bibliography of such contentions would run to many pages. In general, it was held that dope could be a key to individual religious experience, that it could help a given religious community to cohere, and that it could affect the

lives of users in such a way as to effect ethical action (or at least to promote a particular ethical outlook on life). Such claims were supported
in many cases by references to other (traditional) cultures in which the
use of dope for religious purposes has long been accepted (as in the
case of the peyote- and mushroom-related religions in the Americas).

In such religious esteem was dope held that many spoke of it as a
sacrament and contended that it should be used ritually, as would befit
a powerful substance.

> A sacrament is a covenant between man and God and also any
> ritual that corporately grows out of that covenant to express it
> more fully. It can be bread and wine, peyote or mushrooms, a cup
> of tea, LSD, the tobacco used in the sacred pipe, whatever is put
> into the body to connect the world outside with the world within.[52]

This sort of sentiment was fairly common, even if most counterculturists
did not go as far as Tim Leary did and assert that dope should
be used *only* as a sacrament. To most, dope was not *exclusively* a path
to ultimate religious truth, even if providing spiritual experiences was
one of its functions.[53] And that it was a new sacrament did not make it
inherently suspect; indeed, newness gave it a special validity and a special urgency: "Sacraments wear out. They become part of the . . . game.
Treasure LSD while it still works. In 15 years it will be tame, socialized
routine."[54] Or, as the Boston mystic Mel Lyman wrote:

> LSD does what alcohol did when IT was new and what EVERY new
> creation does, it lets a little more light into the darkness of man. It
> is art, it is philosophy, it is education, it is whatever fills the mind
> with more light. . . . It is a trip from the mind to the soul and back
> again, a ROUND trip.[55]

Not all of the counterculture considered the use of dope a predomi-
nantly religious experience, however. In a rather unscientific survey
called "Black Market Research," conducted by underground papers in
New York, Dallas, and Detroit, 38 percent of the respondents in both
New York and Dallas said that their use of dope was at least sometimes
religious, while in Detroit the figure was 87 percent.[56] There were a
few who believed dope would not lead one to deep religious conviction (Paul Krassner once said that LSD provided "a different God that

I didn't believe in"[57]), or whose concerns regarding dope simply fell a long way from anything that should be called "religious" (Tom Wolfe, for example, contrasted the fun-centered approach to dope of Ken Kesey and his secular Merry Pranksters with that of Timothy Leary and the psychedelic religionists[58]). Still, the belief that dope had religious potential was widespread. Leary cited five specific studies as, collectively, having indicated that:

> (1) if the setting is supportive but not spiritual, between 40 to [sic] 75 per cent of psychedelic subjects will report intense and life-changing religious experiences; and that (2) if the set and setting are supportive and spiritual, then from 40 to 90 per cent of the experiences will be revelatory and mystico-religious.[59]

R. E. L. Masters and Jean Houston determined that 96 percent of the 207 subjects in an experiment seeking to describe the content of dope-related religious visions experienced visual religious imagery of some kind;[60] Walter Houston Clark, a veteran psychedelic researcher in the Boston area went even farther, stating, on the basis of one hundred replies to a questionnaire circulated among users of psychedelics, that "So far there is *not one* who has not described some element of religious experience on the questionnaire," and going on to describe many specific testimonies of religious experiences from previously nonreligious individuals.[61] Many countercultural writers agreed with that sort of finding; even though there was virtually no critical analysis of such religiosity, the fact that people experienced it was widely affirmed. Testimonies to that effect were legion; this one was provided by an unidentified writer in the Washington *Free Press*:

> Most of those who have used LSD report that through this drug they have found a spiritual agility and a gracefulness which leads them to believe they have achieved an unusual unification of the mind, the soul and the senses. They also seem to believe that the psychedelic drugs can give them special insight into themselves.[62]

That religious experience could be related to at least some drug experiences would appear to have been demonstrated by Walter N. Pahnke in his "Good Friday" study in which psilocybin was administered to several volunteers, and a placebo to others, in a double-blind experiment in Boston. The experiment took place in the basement of a chapel on Good Friday; the sound of a worship service upstairs was piped in for the volunteers. Employing standard categories which scholars have used to describe the religious experience, Pahnke concluded that those taking the psychedelic chemical had substantially more profound experiences than those receiving the placebo.[63]

The relative lack of analysis of the nature of the psychedelic religious experience by underground writers is problematic. Such analysis as was offered was nearly always analogical, generally comparing psychedelic religious experience to some more conventional religious experience, most frequently to Oriental traditions. Episcopal Bishop James Pike, speaking to a hip audience, contended that the psychedelic and mystical experiences were "identical," since monks fasting, for example, "create chemical changes through vitamin deficiency that lifts [sic] the screen the same way that the drug lifts the screen."[64] Among underground writers, some saw dope as a short-cut to true mysticism (it was said to be capable of "stripping off the sludge which has accumulated on us"[65]); others saw it not as a short-cut, but a related discipline by which one had a chance to explore new sequences of goals.[66] Whatever the nature of the experience, though, there was a very widespread agreement that it was real:

> What's phenomenal about LSD and related mind-changers is that drug technology hasn't just brought us delirium or flashing, fascinating entertainment; it has actually given us something akin to the philosopher's stone. It has discovered a way to mass-produce extreme experience.[67]

Dope was not only seen as important for individual religious experiences, but also as useful for fostering religious community. William C. Shepherd observed that the ritual use of dope produced a very important "sense of social 'belongingness.'"[68] Willie Minzey, the leader of the Shiva Fellowship of the Neo-American Church in San Francisco, saw the religious element of dope best manifested in the concept of Shiva, which he said was revealed "thru joyous group spiritual experience involving the use of psychedelic substances."[69] One communalist wrote of LSD, "We use it as a sacrament within our family structure. . . . We don't take it to ball, to freak out, or trip out. We use it specifically to keep ourselves together."[70] The rituals surrounding dope provided a new basis for group intimacy, and dope itself helped maintain and further that intimacy, its users believed.

Dope religion involved mystical experience; usually it stopped there, but in a few cases it produced in the partaker an ethical imperative. Several countercultural writers maintained that dope was the direct cause (or one direct cause, at least) of the concern in the counterculture for ethical action. Underground papers proclaimed that "Some have discovered LOVE through dope"[71] and as a result "feel as Messiahs, . . . eager to spread their message of salvation from an essentially irreligious, non-humanistic and unesthetic society."[72] And, as in other situations, dope's carryover effect worked here: the ethical insights inspired by dope remained when the high was gone. "Many have noted the tendency of psychedelic users to make major life-changing decisions while under the drug, decisions that are often carried through once the drug wears off," P. G. Stafford noted. Dope gave the user the "opportunity for 'self-transcendence,'" and that quality could, at least in some cases, result in ethical concern and activity.[73]

It should be noted in passing that both scholars and underground writers were well aware that drug-related religious experience has solid historical precedent. In addition to the use of dope in Indian, American Indian, and other cultures,[74] some saw dope in the Judaeo-Christian tradition. Thaddeus and Rita Ashby speculated that peyote may have been among the "vegetables" mentioned in Romans 14:2 and elsewhere.[75] Reading the hip writers, one is reminded of John Allegro's contention that mushrooms were the basis of the Judaeo-Christian tradition, indeed that "Christ" was simply the secret name for the sacred fungus.[76]

But the past here was less important than the present. Quite simply, as one writer put it, "The psychedelic movement is, for me, a holy thing, and it is for a lot of people who are into it.[77]

Awareness of Nature and One's Unity with It. In several instances underground writers advocated the use of dope as a means of communing with nature and understanding the natural order of the world. Nature meant the whole environment, urban as well as rural. As "Paul Scorpio" wrote, "A stone on the curb of my street didn't mean the same to me as a stone in the middle of a forest; it was important to consider the totality: sound, light, absence of human beings, how the stone got there and where it might be tomorrow or ten years from then, etc."[78]

This sense of wonder at nature was connected to the appreciation many hippies cultivated for Native Americans; it was also related to the urgency many hippies felt in wanting to preserve the world's environment. Persons were part of the natural world, and feeling and appreciating that was part of the dope experience.

Dope and Better Sex. Many hip writers valued dope for its alleged heightening of sexual pleasure. The LSD experience was often described as resembling sexual experience in its sensuousness; but beyond that, many believed that dope was a splendid aphrodisiac. Timothy Leary, in a celebrated *Playboy* interview in 1968, made an extravagant version of the claim:

> The three inevitable goals of the LSD session are to discover and make love with God, to discover and make love with yourself, and to discover and make love with a woman. . . . The LSD session that does not involve an ultimate merging with a person of the opposite sex really isn't complete. . . . One of the great purposes of an LSD session is sexual union.
>
> It's socially dangerous enough to say that LSD helps you find divinity and helps you discover yourself. You're already in trouble when you say that. But then if you announce that the psychedelic experience is basically a SEXUAL experience, you're asking to bring the whole middle-class monolith down on your head.[79]

Leary's claim was overstated, but the perceived relation of dope and sex in the counterculture was supported by the Black Market Research studies. 70 percent of the Dallas respondents, 33 percent of those in New York, and an unspecified "high" percentage of both male and female respondents in Detroit said that they engaged in sex while turned on with dope.[80]

That any form of dope is an aphrodisiac is doubtful from a scientific point of view, but insofar as dope (especially marijuana) tends to foster a sense of relaxation and social intimacy, it certainly has the potential to enhance sexual pleasure. In addition, most dope expands the user's perceived sensory awareness; that could logically lead to an increase in experienced sexual pleasure. Marijuana often produces time distortion in the user and thus can give a sense of prolonged orgasm.[81] Whatever the biochemical facts, most hippies were convinced that dope could and did enhance sexuality and pleasure.

Heightening Intimacy, Interpersonal Interaction, and Cooperation. Dope was held to promote a sense of intimacy with the social world just as it did with the natural world. William Braden saw the counterculture as retreating from the metaphysical dualism that for centuries had fostered privatism and individualism. The counterculture, even though it had cultural conflicts with other elements of society, came to maintain that although persons had individual minds and beings, they were nonetheless all related.[82]

Some countercultural writers saw dope as a key to bridging deep cultural chasms. "The new force unleashed by LSD constituted the primary unifying factor in a grouping which ranged from the sometimes violent Hell's Angels motorcycle club to meditating Zen Buddhists," two Philadelphia writers contended.[83] Another writer saw this unity graphically demonstrated in a marijuana smoke-in in New York:

> Psychedelic technology really works, not just as a way to get high, but at the very least, as a way of diminishing friction between people. And, after all the talk of psychedelic revolution, the real, shared experience of the smoke-in contributed to something that all the money or media coverage hippies can marshal couldn't insure. There is peace in the park. If the psychedelic revolution involves even this minimal social transformation, then it has to appeal, in an immediate and living way, to the socio-economic groups that stand to gain through social transformation.[84]

But the community engendered by dope tended to extend only to the initiated. Indeed, that community was by and large at odds with the rest of society: "Drugs leave a feeling of being different from anyone else who does not use drugs and a brotherhood, if only chemical, with those that do."[85] Nonetheless, communal solidarity was part of the overall dope experience. Some believed that the community setting prevented addiction; it was the lonely, the outcasts for whom use turned into abuse and habit.[86]

Dope as a Neutral Tool. The majority of counterculturists argued that dope itself was positive and productive of beneficial experiences, that it both had intrinsic power for good and was used in such a fashion (that is, in supportive groups, for the most part) as to promote positive reactions. A minority of hippies argued, however, that dope was neither good nor bad of itself; it took on meaning and value only as it was used, and the drug's actual role in the overall experience could be seen as quite limited. Andrew Weil has summed up this line of thought well by speaking of dope as an "active placebo" in which the effect is substantially supplied by the user.[87]

Timothy Leary presented a variation on this argument in contending that LSD merely served to assist the user beyond his or her "imprinting," which was a "biochemical event" by which the greater portion of the brain was rendered inaccessible.[88] With his colleagues Ralph Metzner and Richard Alpert he wrote, "Of course, the drug does not produce the transcendent experience. It merely acts as a chemical key—it opens the mind, frees the nervous system of its ordinary patterns and structures. The nature of the experience depends almost entirely on set and setting."[89]

Set meant the preparation of the user, in terms of personality structure and mood at the time; setting meant the environment: the physical surroundings (weather, the atmosphere of the place involved), the social environment (feelings of persons present toward each other), and the cultural environment (the "prevailing views as to what is real").[90]

In this view, the value and benefit of dope are supplied by the user. "It's like fucking, or eating potatoes, or anything else. There are people that hurt themselves using it, and there are people who are better for using it."[91]

Dope Just for Fun. One simple but important argument for the use of dope was that dope was fun. It makes you feel good, the argument went, both while you are high and afterward. As one hip writer put it, "The holiest, happiest, healthiest people I know are those who have used the most dope."[92]

The Black Market Research studies indicated that most dope users saw fun as a major part of it all: 90 percent of the Dallas sample, 51 percent of the New York sample, and an unspecified "high" percentage of the Detroit sample confirmed that having fun was a part of their dope experience.[93] In fact, the studies themselves were criticized by one writer because they attempted to make a semiscientific determination of the ideology of dope, which was contrary to its spirit: "The way of life, for a whole lot of smokers, is just to get high."[94]

The pleasure ethic was not held in especially high esteem in American society in hippie days, at least theoretically, because it conflicted with the Protestant work ethic.[95] So the counterculturists again clashed with the values of the prevailing society. The benchmark of the counterculture was "If it feels good, then do it so long as it doesn't hurt anyone else." According to the hippies, dope, per se, really didn't hurt anyone, and certainly it did not do direct damage to the nonuser. Bad trips were rare, given attention to set and setting; it was nonusers rather than users who were concerned about them. Most of the damage that dope did to society, said the hippies, was caused by oppressive drug laws, not by dope itself. Thus the counterculture believed that pleasure was a perfectly legitimate reason for using dope.

Dope Is Harmless. The counterculture not only maintained that dope was socially harmless, but also that it was not dangerous to the normal person—or at least not more dangerous than the drugs with which society was generally infatuated, such as nicotine, alcohol, amphetamines, barbiturates, and so forth. If we are destined to use drugs anyway, why not use a less harmful rather than a more harmful substance?

The Black Market Research studies indicated that 84 percent of Dallas respondents and 73 percent of New York respondents had never experienced undesirable aftereffects or hangovers from dope.[96] During the heyday of hip a number of physicians and scientists affirmed the relative harmlessness of dope in articles widely printed in the underground press.[97] At least one, the widely read "Dr. Hippocrates" (Eugene Schoenfeld), argued that the notion that LSD was harmful was a distorted idea promoted "by those who oppose new ideas out of fear, ignorance and prejudice. The LSD controversy may well be remembered in history as ranking with the persecution of those who thought the earth was round or that the universe did not really move about the earth."[98] In sum, the hippies believed that a cocktail party was a cesspool far worse than a hip festival, and Grey Line tours were "vastly more deadening and sterile than an LSD trip."[99]

The Medical Usefulness of Dope. The goodness of dope was underscored by its medical potential. When hippies began to use dope, some medical researchers were beginning to believe it useful for the treatment of some mental disorders and, in the case of LSD, treatment of alcoholism.[100]

Enough therapists believed in the clinical usefulness of LSD that in the 1960s they founded the Society of Acid Therapists. Essentially, LSD therapy attempted to help an individual through his or her problems by stripping away the learned perceptual framework that was acquired in the maturation process. In the case of alcoholism, underground press articles often cited scholarly literature to suggest that in some cases LSD apparently helped cure the disease.[101] Marijuana also was held to be useful for various health problems. A Liberation News Service story in 1970 described Army studies that indicated marijuana might be useful medicine for victims of tetanus, migraine, high blood pressure, and sunstroke.[102] Later it became fairly well accepted that marijuana was useful for the relief of glaucoma. Was there anything dope couldn't do?

Dope and Creativity. A key countercultural claim for dope was that it was a great wellspring of creative ideas and action. Writers, musicians, and graphic artists saw dope as inspiring, or even creating, their art. Everyday hippies, as well as professional artists, subscribed to that point of view. In the Black Market Research studies, 54 percent of the Dallas sample, 25 percent of the New York sample, and an unspecified "high" percentage of the Detroit sample indicated that they pursued creative work while high.[103]

Much of that creativity was believed to come directly from the dope high, but perhaps even more was attributed to dope's carry-over effect, the sense that insights gained while high influenced, positively, later activities. So asserted Allen Ginsberg, arguably the foremost countercultural figure in the arts, who characterized marijuana, for example, as "a useful catalyst for specific optical and aural aesthetic perceptions."[104] He continued,

> Drugs were useful for exploring perception, sense perception, and exploring different possibilities and modes of consciousness . . . and useful for composing, sometimes, while under the influ-

ence. Part II of 'Howl' was written under the influence of peyote. . . . 'Kaddish' was written with amphetamine injections.[105]

Most hippie artists did not produce works as powerful as Ginsberg's,
but they enthusiastically shared his belief in the creative powers of
dope.

✳ ✳ ✳ Countercultural Opposition to Dope and Drugs

Despite their general infatuation with dope, many counterculturists saw that the larger drug world did have a downside. There
were, indeed, harmful drugs; good drugs/dope could be used in a destructive manner; and, worse, there were a few unscrupulous souls
around who would use dope for evil purposes, especially for control-
ling others.

Opposition to Harmful Drugs and to Abuse of Dope. Despite the popular
perception that hippies were indiscriminate dopeheads, the counterculture regarded most drugs as harmful, without substantial redeeming social or personal importance. They destroyed the good that dope
had done; they sundered rather than improved the fabric of society.
Almost invariably both heroin and the amphetamines were seen thus;
alcohol was sometimes included. Tim Leary saw dangerous drugs as
the main reason for the fiasco that was the Altamont concert of December 1969 (the large California Rolling Stones concert at which one
person was murdered): "I think it's of great Psycho-pharmacological
interest that the drugs which were most obviously on display at Altamont, particularly around the bandstand were not Psychedelic Drugs
but Speed, Smack, and Booze."[106]
One hip writer contended that "speed and smack will change your
mental attitude. . . . The moment you stick a point in your arm you have
unnaturally altered your whole life."[107] Yet in the case of heroin, the
real culprit was often seen as the federal government and those who
kept heavy drugs illegal, since they unwittingly promoted the crime
in the streets that results from illegal heroin.[108] Allen Ginsberg once
accused the Narcotics Bureau of actually promoting heroin use, since
it meant more appropriations and more jobs within the bureau. More-

over, strong antimarijuana campaigns, such as the ill-fated Operation Intercept, a Nixon-administration program devoted to intercepting marijuana at the border, usually resulted in a massive increase of heroin use, crime, and death by overdose.[109]

Many hip authors condemned amphetamines vigorously. Timothy Leary: "Amphetamines, all of them . . . get you on the wrong track on the way to your energy source. . . . Speed is the symbol of an unturned-on world of growling machinery." [110] Allen Ginsberg: We need a "general declaration . . . contra speedamos. . . . Speed is anti-social paranoid making, it's a drag, bad for your body, bad for your mind . . . a plague on the whole dope industry." [111] David Faber: "Everything about speed is cheap, neon, plastic, ugly Amerika." [112] The warnings were frequent in the underground press; the staff of *Dallas Notes* deemed the problem worthy of a special "Speed Issue" devoted to condemning it.[113]

Many other substances were also considered harmful, and therefore to be condemned, by the underground. In case after case, the underground papers warned readers of bad substances which should be avoided, from cocaine to Hawaiian wood rose.

How exotic did weird highs get? The Spokane *Natural* once took note of accounts in the popular press that hippies were injecting themselves with such strange substances as peanut butter, Aqua Velva, Right Guard, pizza sauce, oil from unhydrogenated peanut butter, mayonnaise, and a brew made from freeze-dried coffee. Such stories, maintained the *Natural*, were simply put-ons:

NO ONE IS STUPID ENOUGH TO DO IT. . . . It's an old head joke. And the heads have been putting on the police so well that it's become a national "new fact."

In all due respect, the police have been the victim of a tremendous hoax. . . . It's the old "big lie" technique—tell a small lie, and it will be disproved, but tell a big lie and everyone will be so overwhelmed that he'll have no choice but to believe it.

And that's the whole point of this article—that ignorant people will believe anything because they don't know enough to refute it. . . . Because [the police] believe that every marijuana user "graduates" to heroin, they have no trouble believing that people really shoot-up peanut butter.[114]

Even good dope was considered subject to misuse. One had to keep one's perspective. Allen Ginsberg again:

> Too many people are taking too many chemicals. . . . There seems to be an entire class of people who take too much of everything. It is like overeating. Acid is really harmless but if you keep taking it too often you have so many different visions of so many different universes you never integrate them.[115]

And some dope was bad because on the street it could be impure: "The major medical problem with acid at the present time is quality control."[116]

So the counterculture favored the use, but not the abuse, of dope and condemned other drugs. For, after all, "That drugs are on occasion misused (i.e., abused) does not significantly detract from their potential benefits."[117]

Opposition to Using Drugs to Influence Others. In the early, formative days of the counterculture, Ken Kesey and his Merry Pranksters performed a number of "acid tests" in which LSD was dissolved in punch which, it became widely believed, people drank without knowing of the presence of the chemical. (Kesey has more recently claimed that dosing without due notice was never actually done.[118]) At the time there was little public countercultural opposition to such practices (indeed, at that time the counterculture hardly existed), but later such activities came to be roundly condemned as, in Tim Leary's words, contrary to "the number one commandment in our religion: Nobody has a right to change my consciousness, I have no right to change your consciousness."[119] When acid testing without notice to partakers occurred at a Los Angeles Easter Sunday love-in in 1968, Art Kunkin, the publisher of the *Free Press*, felt compelled to denounce it, writing, "Turning people on without their knowledge and consent is violating the privacy of another person's body and mind."[120]

In several cases the counterculture saw flashes of what Allen Ginsberg called "a chemical dictatorship."[121] The most prominent case was that of the Charles Manson family, in which drugs were allegedly constantly used as a means of social control.[122] And even though the counterculture disclaimed Manson, saying that he had not "had anything at all to do with the hippie culture,"[123] the inevitable fact was that other would-be Mansons were always nearby, willing and able to prey on the weak.[124] Ed Sanders, in his book on Manson, dwelt at some length on several pain/fear/drug groups that influenced and controlled more than a few people.[125] Some claimed that a similar phenomenon was developing in a group that arose in Boston around Mel Lyman, whose *Avatar* was among the most mystical and cosmic of the underground newspapers. Lyman was given to making spiritually grandiose statements, even going so far in his paper as to claim to be "Christ appearing in this modern day and age. . . ."[126] *Rolling Stone*, in a special series of articles, attacked the Lyman group as potentially more dangerous than the Manson family,[127] although from a later vantage point it must be noted that the Lyman circle is still together and playing an apparently positive role in the several communities where its members live (Mel himself is said to have died several years ago).

And there were other cases of alleged acid fascism. Lucian Truscott told of a huge party near Aspen in 1970 at which a woman, about fifty years of age, was encouraging people to drink her punch which was "alive with acid," apparently gathering them for some sinister purpose under her "complete control."[128] The countercultural bottom line was clear: one had the right to control the expansion or alteration of one's own consciousness without impediment of law, but there could be nothing but total condemnation of those who would commit the most serious drug abuse of all, using drugs to control other persons.

Total Opposition to Dope and Drugs. Dope was part of the very definition of the counterculture; but there were some individuals and groups related to the hippies who, for various reasons, opposed drugs, including dope, entirely. The most common basis for the opposition was religious. Followers of Meher Baba, for example, hip in many ways, frequently opposed the use of dope, claiming that drugs did not give truly new insights, as good religion did, and tended to enhance the ego,[129] or that they helped to perpetuate the illusion that material reality actually existed.[130] (Baba taught that there was no reality except God; one might well ask why drugs mattered at all, since they did not exist.) Most of the Indian gurus admired by hippies similarly opposed all drugs. Swami Satchidananda, for example, reasoned that since it was harder to become a holy person than a doctor or a lawyer, "how can there be a pill to make a man holy when there is no pill to make a doctor or lawyer?"[131]

The counterculture overwhelmingly rejected such thinking, of course. Allen Ginsberg dryly observed, following an argument with the Maharishi Mahesh Yogi, that LSD was actually the key to the Maharishi's success in America, since trippers enlightened by LSD were those open to his message, and that at any rate no matter what the gurus said, the religious value of LSD was utterly obvious to a great many persons.[132]

The other main locus of opposition to all use of dope was the New Left, some of whose activists saw dope as incompatible with the coming revolution. Dope drew persons inward, removing them "from the arena of social consciousness and collective struggle."[133] One writer described the initial reaction of the New Left to the rise of dope use as scorning it as "bread and circuses, the ultimate pacification program."[134]

Others opposed dope for a variety of reasons. Some believed that an adequate high depended on one's state of mind, and could be achieved without dope. David Crosby—ironically, considering his own later history of dependency—once noted that the popular Indian musician Ravi Shankar was always stoned but never used dope.[135]

Others simply found dope a waste of time: "And so you get stoned and grin and giggle and waste away the most joyful, alive years of your life. Talking about drugs, where to get them, how much, how good, who's been busted—never speaking of 'heavy' real things, like nature, art, each other, ecstasy."[136]

Still others saw dope as a product of capitalism, and therefore a product to be avoided if possible. One writer described the "drug hierarchy" as "one of the most capitalistic enterprises to be found anywhere," its customers exploited by "a cruel machine which sneers at revolution as it rakes in profits."[137]

But these arguments were as straws in the wind; the counterculture as a whole loved dope, its psychic staff of life. The few hippies who rejected dope were not influential; nonhippies who tried to make the case against dope were regarded as either lamentable or vicious. When Mike Curb, the young president of MGM records, in 1970 dropped eighteen groups that "advocate and exploit drugs" and encouraged radio stations to refrain from playing songs "with drug-oriented lyrics,"

Rolling Stone denounced his action as a "sick grandstand stunt." It also noted that Curb did not cut his best group, Eric Burdon and War, which was selling a lot of records. Steve Gold, Burdon's manager, replied, "Isn't that the sickest pile of bullshit you ever heard? . . . This must be the last dying gasp of a man that's failed and is on the way out. . . . We're a drug-oriented act and have never tried to hide that."[138]

CHAPTER 3

The Ethics of Sex

Take off your clothes, unless you're cold, and touch each other—yes, even

strangers. Make love—not to one guy or chick who you grab onto and possess

out of fear and loneliness—but to all beautiful people, all sexes, all ages.

—Ron Norman, *Seventy-Nine Cent Spread*, 5 November 1968

We do not announce the "sex orgy." We announce the true spirit of the high holy

act of fucking. People must be free to fuck without molestation, without fear,

without guilt.

—"Om," Berkeley *Barb*, 5–11 June 1970

In its use of dope the counterculture proclaimed freedom of access to mental pleasure. Sex did the same for physical pleasure: free people should express their sexuality as they choose. To the hippies, any special character that sex might have did not mean that it should be restricted; sex was, rather, a range of powerful and wonderful feelings and activities which one should feel free to enjoy at will. No person was to be forced to engage in any sexual activity, but neither was any person required to restrain his or her sexual impulses. Sex was good. Sex was fun. Sex was healthy. And this hip approach to sex revolutionized attitudes, and to some extent practices, in the nation as a whole—at least until the advent of AIDS.

A note from chapter one needs to be repeated here: the heyday of hip came before the widespread dissemination of contemporary feminist thought, and hip writing on sex looks, a quarter-century later, distinctly unenlightened. Sex roles were often traditional in the counterculture, and when feminist ideas first began to be raised in progressive circles, around 1968,[1] many male hippies turned out to be as disinclined to give women equal rights and privileges as males elsewhere in society. A fair number of the early new feminists were influenced by the counterculture. One can argue that they tended to take seriously talk of equality, which heretofore had been conceived in class and racial terms; and perhaps the gap between expansive hippie rhetoric and the disinclination of many hip males to liberate themselves from old sexual thinking helped some spur some of the new feminists into revolt.

In any event, sexual liberation was presented in the underground press in largely male-oriented terms; the chief point of the sexual "revolution" was male pleasure. The counterculture bloomed before either contemporary feminism or homosexual activism amounted to much; *Roe vs. Wade* was still years down the road as well, and devastating disease was not much in the picture (yes, there were venereal diseases, but the common ones were easily curable). Many former hippies reading their old utterances on sexual liberation might find them obsolete today.

✳ ✳ ✳ The Broad Case for Liberated Sexuality

The concept of free sexuality is hardly new. There have been advocates of liberated sexuality throughout the ages, starting with the ancients, through such phenomena as the "complex marriage" of the Oneida Community in the nineteenth century, to such modern advocates of sexual liberty as Dr. Albert Ellis.

Sex, in the counterculture, was fun and free, certainly more fun to engage in than to write about. "Anyone who has time to write articles protesting sexual mores should fuck more," one hip author intoned.[2] At the same time, sex was understood as an expression of humanness, a means of human communication that operated at the deepest levels of being. It was the "human touch, without conquest or domination, and it obviates self-consciousness and embarrassed speech."[3] As Leah Fritz of Berkeley wrote,

> As for sex—like eating, like walking in fresh air, like all human activity—it should recreate us, help us to find one another, make us real, and tangible as the earth. It should put us together again, body and soul, male and female, in harmonious intercourse.[4]

Pleasure and communication, then, were the two main touchstones of countercultural sexuality. To a lesser degree, sex was also held to be revolutionary.[5] As one countercultural author put it,

> Sexual repression is counter-revolutionary. It is the denial of our most basic self. When sex is both repressed and sublimated it is the driving force of civilization. "Don't let those slaves fuck around, man, we've got a pyramid to build."
>
> Fortunately, as we all know, civilization is teetering on the brink.[6]

The hippies were in the vanguard of a revolutionary smashing of sexual taboos. Concern over promiscuity, opposition to masturbation, demanding that sex be strictly marital, and guilt feelings over being sexually active have clearly decreased sharply in American culture as a whole over the last two or three decades, and the hippies were among the first to occupy the turf of sexual liberation.

What was once known as promiscuity was rampant in the counter-culture, but it was no longer shameful or hidden. Now it was time to redefine terms. "Don't apply descriptions of promiscuity to yourself. It's the first step toward involving yourself in endless attempts to prove those tags as self-definitive. And that's a pile of bull-shit, lover, you don't deserve to bear."[7]

The counterculture saw the marital contract as irrelevant to sex. "A legal contract for a sexual relationship is, if not out of date, at least beside the point for most of us."[8] Some went further, maintaining that sexually exclusive marriage itself was a manifestation of what was wrong with Western sexuality:

> There is no reason why [sex] should not be shared. It not only brings you closer to your friends but it also brings you closer to your wife or husband. The concerned Christian I am sure would not believe this; but consider the Eskimos; they were invariably described as the happiest people on the earth until we gave them "virtue." Now they too have chastity and adultery and jealousy. Instead of happiness they are as glum as the concerned Christians and with the same hang-ups.[9]

Guilt over one's noncoercive sexual activities was declared out of bounds.

There are people, young and old, who enjoy their own sexuality and enjoy sharing sex, with no guilt feelings. They like their bodies. They like other people's bodies. They are not self-conscious of *bodies* . . . they are not *afraid* to express themselves when they want to.

It is *great* to make love and not feel guilty about it.[10]

Since "there is no activity which is in itself sick,"[11] countercultural condemnation of any voluntary sexual act was hard to find. The *Village Voice*, for example, gave space to advocates of sadism and masochism as well as to those of asexuality and virginity.[12]

Some favored masturbation. "Masturbation is not something to do just when you don't have a lover. It's different from, not inferior to, sex for two."[13] And "Honest masturbation is a lot healthier than a dishonest lay."[14] Others liked transvestism.[15] Homosexuality was entirely acceptable. Group sex and sexual party games? No problem.[16] The hip credo ruled the world of sex: If it feels good, do it, as long as it doesn't hurt anyone else.[17]

But liberated sexuality in the counterculture went beyond the simple level of freedom of choice and orgasmic gratification. Some argued that sex was far more than simple copulation, that regarding sex simply as an act of ejaculation was symptomatic of the "sensual sterility in the Western culture."[18] A better ideal was that of total sexuality in which, as Don H. Somerville put it, there were several reproductive organs but only one sex organ—the whole body.[19] Quite a few hippies became interested in the writings of Wilhelm Reich, who promoted a "complete" orgasm that released tension and gave pleasure throughout the body.[20]

✳ ✳ ✳ Homosexuality

One of the most important components of the hip-era sexual revolution was the rise of public gay consciousness, and the underground press gave considerable publicity and support to that phenomenon. Although one cannot exactly argue that the hippies spawned the gay liberation movement, it is fair to say that hip tolerance of sexual activity contributed to the atmosphere in which the gay revolution could emerge.

Homosexuals and their supporters wrote frequently in the underground press, making a broadly based case for an ethics of homosexuality[21]; their arguments were not unlike those of the heterosexual liberationists. There were five main lines of argument:

1. Homosexuality is natural and good. "To deny the rightful existence of homosexuality is a perversion of the laws of nature. . . . People are capable of being gratified sexually by any person. . . . To limit sexual contact to male-female genital play is dumb."[22] Many writers noted that there have been many times and places in history in which homosexuality was not only accepted, but even preferred; the ancient Greeks had a proverb, a hip writer averred: "For children a woman, for true love, a boy."[23] Some pointed out that homosexuality could provide an essential social service to an overpopulated world, since it was a system of total birth control.[24] It also helped straighten out sex roles, offering an alternative to the "present patriarchal patterns of male-female heterosexuality."[25]

2. A person has a right to free sexual choice. Although relatively few hippies said that homosexuality was the *only* good sex, it was a choice as legitimate as any other. While "the whole world is not gay,"[26] hippies stood for nothing if not freedom of choice.

3. One should not have to hide his or her sexual preferences. Homosexuality wasn't wrong, and it shouldn't have to be secret. Gays needed to "stop mimicking straights; stop censoring ourselves."[27] "Our message is that homosexual love is good. Holding hands is not inappropriate."[28] It was in the spirit of openness that one group of California homosexuals devised a short-lived plan to take over Alpine County, a sparsely populated piece of the Sierra Nevada, in 1970. Why should there not be an openly gay junior college, a gay museum, gay housing, gay health services, gay public officials, gay publications? Homosexuals should have the freedom to live openly that others have.[29]

4. All private acts between consenting adults should be legal.[30] Why was it that two men could get into a boxing ring and hurt each other with people watching, but not have private love? Why was oral copulation illegal? "Blow jobs are beautiful. They are natural, basic, simple, fun. . . . Something so important as that . . . should be legalized."[31]

5. Social discrimination against homosexuals should end. Under prevailing conditions, homosexuals were not only subject to occasional unprovoked physical attacks; they were restricted seriously in security clearance, military service, citizenship, and employment, among other things. Homosexuals paid taxes, but "the only things we get for our taxation are undesirable discharges and bad employment records when we are discovered in government jobs. Local banks will accept homosexual money but fire homosexual employees. Oil companies like homosexuals to have credit cards but dislike giving them paychecks."[32] As Supreme Court Justice William O. Douglas was reported to have written, "Homosexuals have, in this century, been members of both Congress and the Executive, and have served with distinction."[33] It was time, according to the counterculture, to legitimize free sexual preference. In sum, "All we hell-raising homosexuals want is humanness. And we will have humanness when every man understands he is more similar to than different from his fellowmen and is willing to contribute a little effort to insure the same quality of life for everyone in the community."[34]

When a militant new phase of the gay rights movement took shape in the wake of a police raid on the Stonewall bar in Greenwich Village in June 1969, the new revolutionaries found a sympathetic audience among the hippies and, often, a soapbox in the underground press. A few weeks after the Stonewall raid, for example, the New York *Rat* approvingly reported the formation of the Gay Liberation Front and announced the platform of the new militancy:

> We are a revolutionary homosexual group of men and women formed with the realization that complete sexual liberation for all people cannot come about unless existing social institutions are abolished. . . . We are creating new social forms and relations, that is, relations based upon brotherhood, cooperation, human love, and uninhibited sexuality. Babylon has forced us to commit ourselves to one thing . . . revolution.[35]

* * * Nudity

Nudity was part of the counterculture's new sexuality. The public was first made widely aware of countercultural nudity at the Woodstock festival, press reports of which rather luridly featured mass skinny-dipping, but the phenomenon was more pervasive than that. In part, the counterculture simply revived classic nudist philosophy, which argued that clothes hindered interpersonal communication, that going without clothing was natural, and that nudity was fun. But the counterculture generally stopped about there, rejecting "Establishment" nudism's emphasis on physical exercise and proscription of public sexuality in the nudist context.

Graphic representation of nudity was a prominent part of the underground press. Photos of naked women and men were common, and underground cartoons contained depictions of nudity that ranged from the explicit to the depraved. The underground comic books ("comix") were often fixated on sex and nudity, determined to smash the prevailing society's taboos, to the extent that in a fair number of cases they had little redeeming social importance.

Nudity was in keeping with the counterculture's love of bodily pleasure; and, as such, it was not so much exhibitionism and voyeurism as it was appreciation of the total body. In fact, countercultural nudity proposed to liberate persons, through overexposure, from excessive concern with genitalia. As a hip writer put it,

It is in the interest of any culture to perpetuate a special excitement on the part of its members in the genitals. The propaganda runs that "real sexuality" exists finally in the groin. . . . The genitals are judged to be ugly [and therefore distinguished] from the rest of the body which is potentially beautiful and so not particularly sexual. . . . Had the genitals been left uncovered they would have blended naturally with the rest of the body. . . . All parts of all healthy bodies would have been equally well suited for pleasure. . . . Thus . . . every unveiling of the genitals to public inspection will upset the limiting fixation that the genitals are somehow each person's own piece of ugly private property. Similarly, every revelation of the genitals will disturb the esthetic cop-out away from the need to get pretty in the eye before one can get warm in the groin. (The various sensory mixtures that will result include getting pretty in the groin and warm in the eye.) When the genitals lose their special significance then people will cease to fear them and so cease to need to build special monuments to them. It is because they are hidden that they are ugly and dirty.[36]

Where did the countercultural passion for nudity originate? LeRoy Moore, Jr., argued that it all began with the civil rights demonstrations, in which the physical importance of bodies for strategic purposes was stressed:

> This tactic of bodily presence spread to a multitude of causes and a variety of forms ranging from passive nonviolence to provocative convulsions born of frustration and despair. But in every case the effect has been to provide by means of a bothersome presence of bodies a tangible witness of value (or disvalue) of particular bodies and public rebuke for those who victimize the body.[37]

A different case might be made for the influence of *Playboy*, which a decade before the beginnings of the counterculture had broken the taboo in an openly available publication. Although the counterculture generally derided the plastic nudity of an airbrushed Playmate, *Playboy* nonetheless made the important innovation of taking nudity and sex out of the closet. It placed (male) sexual pleasure in a context of fashionable middle-class living and, by filling the magazine otherwise with good works of fiction and nonfiction, implicitly said that nudity and a concern for bodily pleasure were not incompatible with the workings of the mind. Many hippies criticized *Playboy's* exploitation of women, but in a sense it was the counterculture that put Hugh Hefner's theories into practice. Although by the latter days of the counterculture the emerging feminist critique was pointing out the bias and exploitiveness of the *Playboy* approach, the magazine's role in the development of countercultural sexual ethics seems unavoidable.

The counterculture's advocacy of nudity, as of liberated sexuality generally, rested primarily on grounds of fun and freedom: nudity was fun per se, and it was a symbol of the free lifestyle advocated by hippies. It wasn't an end in itself, nor was it a therapeutic tool, as it was in certain encounter groups. It was, rather, a simple enjoyment of a given time and place. In the words of LeRoy Moore, Jr., hip nudity said, "Here I am; see me; so what is new?" It extolled "a loss of a certain sense of shame, accompanied by a sense of wonder and playfulness."[38] Thus one underground writer could say,

> Nudity on a beach, meadow or forest is an experience that is very much apart from sexuality. It is a communion with all of the gods' creations. It is a pure animal delight in the freedom of the body wildly playing in the elements. It is an aesthetic joy in the beauty of the human form. It is one of life's richest and most pleasurable experiences. . . .
>
> This growth is heartening in a world of silly hang-ups. Nudity makes one free of hang-ups. One becomes a part of the wind and water, and once this is experienced one can never wear a bathing-suit again.[39]

Nudity was also held to stand for the sort of freedom that should be basic in a free society: "If I have any liberty at all, I have the liberty to be naked. . . . If the State shall deny me this right, then it may deny me any other right it sees fit. . . ."[40]

The fact that nudity was a cultural taboo meant that it could provide a vehicle for dissent. Sometimes the dissent was generalized, as in the case of public nude-ins.[41] Nudity outraged the majority of citizens, and that was reason enough for it. As Richard Neville wrote, it "communicates a commitment to total rehabilitation of social values, it makes news, and surprisingly discourages arrest."[42] So mass nudity provided a vehicle for collective nose-thumbing at society. That was the sort of feeling that Louis Abolafia tapped when he appeared at nude-ins around the country in 1968, running as the naked candidate for president on the slogan, "What have I got to hide?"

But nudity as dissent could also be more specific than that. In some cases, hip mothers stripped their children to keep them out of public schools.[43] In a well-publicized incident at Grinnell College, six women and four men undressed in the presence of a representative of *Playboy* to protest that magazine's exploitation of the human body. ("Playboy Magazine is a money-changer in the temple of the body. Playboy substitutes fetishism for honest appreciation of the endless variety of human forms."[44]) The Shiva Fellowship, which held many nude meetings in public parks in San Francisco, advocated "immediate nudity as resistance to hostile cops at public demonstrations. . . ."[45]

Indeed, there were many proposals for confrontational nudity (most of which never materialized), sponsored by such groups as the Neo-Naked Noisy Committee for Peace and Love and the Bare Breasts for Peace Brigade. In a manner reminiscent of the Doukhobors, the Canadian religious sectarians who have sometimes taken off their clothes as an act of defiance at times of conflict with the government, the hippies found that nudity can interfere effectively with the usual procedures of the civil authorities.

✳ ✳ ✳ Sacramental/Symbolic/Ritual Uses of Sex

Although the predominant attitude toward sex in the counterculture was supportive of sexual freedom on grounds of pleasure and individual free choice,[46] there were some who saw liberated sexuality as having a larger significance. Free sex and nudity could lead to a "feeling of communion," to an exhiliration that "is such that it comes close to supernaturalism."[47]

One movement for liberated, sacramental sex was the Om United Nude Brigade. Richard Thorne, a former president of the Sexual Freedom League, proclaimed that he was "the living personification of Om, who is . . . the creator of the universe,"[48] and had manifested himself "to announce universal nudity and the holiness of copulation. . . . We must abstain from selfishness, jealousy, possessiveness, but not copulation."[49] The Brigade came to public attention in a series of public marches, in which Thorne's followers paraded in the nude. It claimed divine authority: "If dicks are lewd, if pussies are obscene, then God is lewd; God is obscene. For it is God who made the dick to fit the pussy; God who made the pussy to fit the dick."[50]

Another group that decorated its sexual thinking with religious trappings was the Shiva Fellowship (and its successor, the Psychedelic Venus Church), which held many public nude meetings, several of which resulted in arrests.[51] One of its "rituals" was oral sex, which it called a "genital sacrifice."[52]

Some even argued for sacramental sex in traditional religious settings; after all, had there not once been ritual prostitution in the Temple in Jerusalem? One Gay Liberation Front member writing in the Berkeley *Tribe* described a spontaneous male homosexual act on an altar, quoting one of the participants:

> I began making love to him, kissing his cock and balls all over. Then I went down on his beautiful cock with my mouth and tongue working it.
>
> Then I felt him come. I really felt it, and tasted it. I've never felt closer in sex than I did at that moment. There was a high mystical energy level. . . .
>
> It was much more meaningful to drink the sweet juice of a human being than the juice of a grape at the altar.

And the other participant in this particular act concurred in its religious significance: "I had mixed feelings about it, even while Steve and I were having sex. But, as it continued, I realized that this was the highest form of worship and felt good about it."[53]

✳ ✳ ✳ The Real-World Concerns

Although the counterculture generally approached sex from a point of view of fun and individual free choice, mundane reality was never far away: not everyone wanted sex to be whimsical, and things like diseases and birth control were parts of the equation that one ignored at one's peril.

The case against the clap. One result of the sexual revolution was the spread of venereal disease to near-epidemic proportions.[54] The clap was, as one writer put it, "one of the hangups of the new morality."[55] The counterculture's reaction to the problem did not involve any renunciation of free and widespread sex, but generally reflected the obvious wisdom that pertained to it: get treatment immediately, tell any person who might be infected, and take reasonable precautionary measures where that is possible. Cooperating with public health officials in this case was eminently reasonable. "Don't think fink! You're doing your friends a favor. It's the only way to stop the spread of the disease."[56]

The case for sex with love. A new sexual era or no, some counterculturists still found sex best within a context of love and concern for the partner. Sex was less than ideal, these persons said, when it was engaged in casually, without real concern for the other person, or under the outdated system of male domination and female submission.[57]

Timothy Leary called into question the whole matter of labeling widespread, uninhibited sexual contact "sexual freedom":

> I think . . . that what's called "sexual freedom" in the United States (which goes along with promiscuity) is just a reaction to Puritan heritages and is not a way of life that's going to stand up as spiritually centered. Infidelity, of course, occurs in large cities and capitals of empires, for when there's boredom, when the spiritual thread has been lost, then you find what you had in Babylon and in Rome and in Athens. Promiscuity can only exist in a city. . . . In a small tribal community the challenge and also the necessity is to make it within the stable relationship, and then you find that the whole thing is within one woman anyway.
>
> [Promiscuity is] an ideal to which all of us honestly respond. I think it takes a tremendously high level of consciousness to pull that off, and there is an incredible opportunity here for cop-outs and for egocentricity and for dishonesty.[58]

So in the quest for a new sexual ethic, some tempered absolute freedom: sex in the meaningful context of love could be better than sex that was casual and transitory.

Birth Control and Abortion. Birth control was an obvious necessity in the world of liberated sexuality. Thus the hip literature on the subject mainly discussed relative efficacy and safety of various methods, not the rightness or wrongness of birth control itself.[59]

Abortion was not quite so clear-cut. Generally, abortion was regarded as the most logical solution to unwanted pregnancy, but the hippies, like just about everyone else, found it the least attractive form of birth control. Advocacy of freedom of choice prevailed; by December 1968, a female counterculturist writing in *Buffalo Chip* was outlining what soon became the position of the nascent women's movement: a woman's body is her own, and she should be free to obtain an abortion when she wishes to.[60] The founding of the National Association for the Repeal of Abortion Laws in 1969 got favorable reviews in the underground press. In September of that year, the New York *Rat* published a cover story that provided a detailed guide to getting an abortion despite the prevalence of generally restrictive laws—reminding readers, however, that "No matter how relaxed you feel about having to face an abortion, it's still a really shitty hassle and more expensive than you can easily afford."[61] Within a few months, the critique of the status quo on abortion was becoming more polished and incisive; a *Rat* piece by the Women's Liberation Health Collective related some illegal-abortion horror stories and proposed a program for reform—research on the best and safest abortion methods, making abortions available without charge, and so forth.[62]

A minority of counterculturists, however, resisted free choice. (In what was perhaps a portent for the future of the abortion debate, most of the hip writers who announced their demurral from the choice position were male.) Ken Kesey was one who supported abortion only to save the life of the mother, arguing that society needed to care about everyone, including "the un-dead old [and] the un-born young." As he put it, "Abortions are a terrible karmic bummer."[63] Similarly Stephen Gaskin, the founder and leader of the Farm, the archetypal hippie commune in Tennessee, was so opposed to abortion that for years the Farm had a standing offer: a pregnant woman could come to the Farm, receive room, board and health care, have the baby delivered, leave the baby at the Farm if she chose to, and still be free to reclaim the child at any future date—all without charge.[64] For Kesey, Gaskin, and the minority they represented, the single fabric of life was not to be torn.

✳ ✳ ✳ Orgies and Organized Free Sex

Another minority argued that orgies had a place in the new sexuality. One writer argued that orgies provided an outlet for the "non-ordinary sexual inclinations which we all possess," that orgies were harmless, that they helped to break down social barriers, that they helped create community spirit, that they were beneficial to one's private sex life, and that they were revolutionary.[65]

Most hippies did not condemn orgies, but neither were they attracted to organized sex, since the hip spirit of liberated sex was one of sponta-

neity, not sex with as many partners as possible. Many hip authors criticized the organized, impersonal "swinging" which they identified as a
manifestation of middle-class shallowness—conduct utterly inferior to
the caring relationships, or at least honest pleasure, the counterculture
advocated.

But the line between personal liberated sexuality and orgies could
be hard to draw. The Sexual Freedom League embodied the ambi-
guity. It had been founded with a hip orientation, scorning "double
standards between the sexes, . . . out-dated sex laws on the books, and
the continuance of hypocritical morality and diseducation on the subject of sex."[66] In its early days the SFL expressed a desire to "spread new
ideas and living concepts" and "to have fun."[67] "The Sexual Freedom
League puts a large emphasis on pleasure NOW, but we feel that if pleasure is the end product of the sexually free society, it is also legitimate
to insist on our prerogatives to enjoy that pleasure now."[68]

Though the SFL was founded in hippie spontaneity, it quickly attracted followers from outside the counterculture, and its orientation
shifted somewhat as a result. It became Establishmentarian—indeed,
it became SFL, Inc.—and became hung up on sexual frequency and
technique, concepts that were hardly spontaneous. Sex in the SFL ultimately became boring, to the point that some of its members decided
that "screwing isn't what they want all the time. Many men at parties
are getting a thrill just cuddling with the women."[69] By then, however,
most hippies were gone from the SFL. Organized free sex was not the
countercultural way.

✳ ✳ ✳ Sex and Drugs

Sex was the essence of one of the hip arguments for dope, as
we have seen: dope was good because, among other things, it enhanced
sexual experience. Over and over again the countercultural writers saw
sex and dope as synergistic. Dope helped persons expand their erotic
horizons, to realize that lovemaking did not consist of orgasm alone.
Timothy Leary summed up the dope/sex connection thus:

The key energy in our revolution is erotic. . . . The sexual revolution is not just part of the atmosphere of freedom that is gener-

ating within the kids. I think it is the center of it. The reason the psychedelic drugs, particularly marijuana, are so popular, is because they turn on the body. I'll say flatly that the meaning and central issue of the psychedelic experiences is erotic exhilaration.[70]

✳ ✳ ✳ Opposition to "Liberated" Sexuality, Especially the Kind Focused on Male Pleasure

There was always a loyal minority on sexual issues among the hippies. The most common critiques came from the emerging women's movement, some of whose advocates saw freewheeling sexual relationships simply as an extension of the male-dominated sexuality of American society at large. The most extreme position in the late 1960s came from SCUM, the Society for Cutting Up Men, whose manifesto began,

> Life in this society being, at best, an utter bore and no aspect of society being at all relevant to women, there remains to civic-minded, responsible, thrill-seeking females only to overthrow the government, eliminate the money system, institute a complete automation and destroy the male sex.[71]

But many rhetorically more moderate women simply advocated withdrawing from the sexual revolution insofar as it involved masculine predominance. "Free" sexuality, like any other kind, "carries with it an unwarranted domination by the man, of the woman, which injures both,"[72] a hip southern female wrote. Another woman was more blunt: "The talk of love is profuse but the quality of relationships is otherwise. . . . The idea of sexual liberation for the woman means she is not so much free to fuck as to get fucked over. . . . Our mothers could get a home and security, a prostitute—money, but a hippie woman is bereft of all that."[73] So some simply felt a need to withdraw from the sexual revolution until the basis for heterosexual relationships was changed for the better.

It was at about this time that lesbianism gradually entered public discussion. The argument was simple and direct: it was difficult to find a truly liberated male who treated his partner "as a HUMAN BEING, not just a piece of meat. This is virtually impossible in our society," and therefore the alternative was female homosexuality, which "eliminates the necessity of tolerating male chauvinism in our lives without giving up the need for meaningful love relations."[74] "Isn't love between equals healthier than sucking up to an oppressor?"[75]

All of this was new and tentative in hippie days; the women's movement was just beginning to gather steam. By 1968 the phrase *Women's Liberation Movement* was beginning to appear in the underground press as well as in the larger society. Late that year the New York *Rat* covered a feminist demonstration staged by the radical group WITCH (Women's International Terrorist Conspiracy from Hell), whose marchers exorcised money from the financial district and protested exploitive burlesque houses in downtown New York.[76] Hippies were slow to become enlightened, but probably not more so than any other major group in society. Indeed, hip openness about sex probably contributed importantly to the discussion—to the fact that lesbianism, for example, could now be talked about publicly. As late as 1970, it was still only in the underground press that the general public could read a lesbian's speculation that "Maybe after the revolution, people will be able to love each other regardless of skin color, ethnic origin, occupation, or type of genitals."[77]

As I have suggested above, it can be argued that hip culture itself played an important role in the rise of the new feminism. Much of the early feminist press in the late 1960s had distinctly countercultural graphics, makeup, and rhetorical tone; there was, for example, a clearly countercultural sauciness to *Everywoman*, a Los Angeles feminist paper founded in May 1970 and given to running articles with titles like "Hymens for Husbands."[78] Hip topics were addressed from a feminist perspective in many of the feminist papers, as in a Baltimore paper's article "Women and Rock: Sexism Set to Music."[79]

In one bold move, an entire major underground paper suddenly went feminist. On 24 January 1970, a group of militant women, some of them staffers of the paper, occupied the offices of and took over the New York *Rat*, announcing that "the culture has got to be revolutionary as surely as the revolution has got to be cultural."[80] The first issue under the new management contained "Goodbye to All That," a manifesto by Robin Morgan, which was reprinted many times elsewhere— Abe Peck, who has provided a good chronicle of the takeover, calls her essay "the shot heard round the Left."[81] Thereafter the paper was run permanently by the women's collective, dropping the previously comprehensive cultural side of the coverage in favor of radical feminism and New Left politics generally. Morgan's polemic set the tone: "Goodbye to Hip Culture and the so-called Sexual Revolution, which has functioned toward women's freedom as did the Reconstruction toward former slaves—reinstituted oppression by another name."[82]

Feminism and women's concerns were not the only sticks in the spokes of the sexual revolution. Sexual liberationist Jefferson Fuck Poland wrote of three other anti–free-sex influences: what he termed religious fanaticism, especially that of the Hare Krishnas, whose movement was nearly celibate; heroin use ("Junkies rarely ball, unless for cash to buy junk. Heroin provides an orgasmic feeling of its own while suppressing sexual desire"); and methedrine use ("While speed doesn't always eliminate sex, it often does so"). Poland theorized that this antisexuality came from "ten years of failure in the Movement for peace, love and racial brotherhood," which had made many former true believers bitter cynics who rejected loving relationships and, as part of the process, turned to mysticism, violence, or antisexual drugs.[83]

Some argued that the sexual revolution was itself antisexual, at least in its more extreme phases. Tom Hayden once castigated the Berkeley *Barb* and, by extension, other aggressively free-sex underground papers as being decadent rather than liberated:

> The Barb only appears to make a break with these repressive [sexual] patterns. There is a sexual attitude in the Barb which seems to suppose that whatever is taboo in America should be celebrated by radicals. But there is such a thing as sexual decadence which should be uninteresting, while not being taboo, to radicals. The Barb reveals this decadence in its sexual focus. The Barb represents a hip version of the morality of the Dirty Old Man, rather than exploring real alternatives to America's sexual neurosis.[84]

Another hip author saw the new sexuality as actually only an increasing narcissism, which was really a new and extreme victorianism in which physical requirements for sexual partners became increasingly exacting. Sex ceased to be pursued for its own sake; it was sought for ego inflation.[85]

Those who had reservations about uninhibited sexuality, however, were a decided minority. Underground writing as a whole put if-it-feels-good-do-it sex in the pantheon alongside peace, love, dope, and rock and roll.

CHAPTER 4

The Ethics of Rock

Rock music is one of the most exciting phenomena of our times. At its best in concert it is complete synesthesia, combining all of the arts and appealing to several levels of appreciation at once—emotional, intellectual, physical and metaphysical.

—Ron Jarvis, *Space City!*, 17–30 January 1970

Sound, like sex and the magic weeds, is a turn-on.

—Tom Sayles, *East Village Other*, 19 August–1 September 1967

Rock and roll was as integral to the counterculture as were dope and sex. Rock swayed a generation both physically and emotionally; the hippies lived and breathed it and believed that it was the most important new musical form to come along in centuries. As Chester Anderson put it, rock "engages the entire sensorium, appealing to the intelligence with no interference from the intellect. Extremely typographic people are unable to experience it."[1]

The point of this chapter is not to analyze the appeal of rock to a generation of American youth, but to look at the ways in which the music influenced the feelings and behavior of its devotees and to see why hippies regarded a musical genre as pivotal to the generational rebellion. Insofar as this chapter is rational, it will—the hippies would have said—miss dealing with the real power of rock, since the music was preeminently something to be experienced and could not be explained entirely rationally. To the hippies, rock was not just sound; it was part and parcel of a way of life, and its ethical dimensions were therefore substantial.

The underground press during the flowering of hip focused overwhelmingly on rock, but folk music was also important to the countercultural musical scene. Folk was the music of cultural rebellion until around 1966 or even later, when the Beatles began to take on mythic significance as interpreters of the culture, new specifically hip rock bands (The Grateful Dead, for example) began to appear, and Bob Dylan incorporated rock into his previously folkish music. Earlier 1960s folk music (Joan Baez, Dylan) continued to be played on hippies' stereos. The counterculture had little sense of history, so many hippies undoubtedly were not concerned with the folk roots of their music. But certainly the folk revival of the 1950s and early 1960s cultivated the ground for the advent of rock. The protest music of Pete Seeger, Phil Ochs, and a host of others was full of peace and justice themes as well as loaded with distrust of the cultural Establishment. As rock historian Geoffrey Stokes points out, folk was a critical catalyst for sixties rock because it bridged the musical gap between the fifties and the sixties. The originally pioneering, revolutionary rock of the fifties had given way by the early sixties to musical styles represented by the likes of the Beach Boys on one hand and Andy Williams on the other. "Faced with the choice between teen and treacle," Stokes writes, "a lot of young people turned to folk music."[2] And from the energized folk scene major portions of the new rock emerged.

✳ ✳ ✳ Rock as a Cultural Language

Dope usually involved inward experiences. Liberated sex in most cases involved interpersonal relationships on a one-to-one basis. Rock, however, was communal, and thus it provided a medium for cultural communication. "Rock music," Ron Jarvis wrote, "is responsible more than any other single factor in spreading the good news. For joy and ecstasy is the essence of rock."[3] Marshall McLuhan, whose ideas circulated widely in the counterculture, reminded us that in our time the content of communication could not be separated from its means of propagation, and that went in spades for rock. Rock's content was important, but so, intangibly, was rock itself.

Rock and roll is the music of RIGHT NOW, every minute, pounding and screaming at your head, twisting inside your belly, pulling you up off your ass to GIVE IT UP and let energy flow through your cells and into the air so you can be FREE again.[4]

People need music to live. We believe that and act on it, all ways. Only straight people—honkies—think music is superfluous, that it doesn't make any difference what you listen to, and their lives demonstrate their ignorance. Music shapes us and makes us whole, as we would never be without it. We have to have it. There's no way you can get around it. For our generation music is the most vital force in most of our lives.[5]

Several features of rock set it apart from other types of music, thus effecting its power. The most basic feature was its incessant rhythm, the driving 4/4 beat. That rhythm demanded dancing, so rock was physical. Rock was sexual; concerts always featured sensuous dress and performances, both from the musicians and from the fans. High amplification was part of the whole, and so were the lyrics which, as with any successful vocal music, expressed the values and concerns of their listeners.

Most counterculturists, however, had no time for even such simple bits of analysis. Rock was a totality, one infused with power. Rock fueled the cultural revolution because it was immediate, spontaneous (at least to the listener), and total. The fact that the lyrics carried a message wasn't the central point. One could dance to it, but one hip writer wrote, "it doesn't care about the artificiality of merely being heard."[6] John Sinclair got to the heart of things:

> Rock and roll is the great liberating force of our time. Its most beautiful aspect is that it gets to millions of people every day, telling them that they can dance and sing and holler and scream and FEEL GOOD even when they have to listen to all those jive commercials and death news reports all around the music, everything's gonna be all right as soon as EVERYBODY GIVES IT UP![7]

Some hip analysts tried to figure out just where that power came from. Chester Anderson, for example, suggested that bass notes were experienced as localized vibrations in the abdomen; that rock rhythms affected the heart, skeletal muscles, and motor nerves; that long, open chords lowered the blood pressure, while crisp, repeated ones raised it; and that melodies affected the larynx, which autonomously subvocalized with rock lyrics.[8] Most counterculturists, however, were content to let it be.

Rock, of course, used modern technological equipment, which made it something of a countercultural paradox—after all, wasn't this a back-to-basics, simple-living movement? The answer had to be that rock transcended its technology and merchandising, that the spiritual guidance of rock was independent of state-of-the-art equipment. Rock was more than the sum of its electronic parts. The danger was always there that it might become "too rational, too business-like, and too orderly," given its merchandising.[9] But rock had the inherent power to overcome the limitations that such a structure might place on it. Indeed, without such power it wouldn't have been *rock*, but just noise.[10]

✳ ✳ ✳ Rock and Dope

Charles Reich argued in *The Greening of America* that dope was "an integral part of the musical experience," and he found little argument among counterculturists.[11] Certainly the conjunction of drugs and music was nothing new under the sun; jazz musicians, for example, had been using various drugs, from marijuana to heroin, for decades before the hippies appeared. Thus the counterculture simply expanded on its musical heritage when it created acid rock, music that was intimately related to cherished dope. After *Sgt. Pepper*, the seminal album of acid rock, rock and dope could not be separated. Most musicians, for quotation in public, had to deny that music and dope were interrelated, but the truth was closer to Ringo Starr's comment that dope "made a lot of difference to the type of music and the words," providing new musical styles and new subject matter for lyrics.[12]

Part of dope's impact on rock was realized through its influence on composers and musicians, but just as important was its influence on listeners, who of course determine what will survive in the marketplace. Listening to music high wasn't the same as listening to the same music straight; music with a special clarity and resonance, to a substance-affected mind, would triumph and did. Dope's carry-over effect was held to be operative here as elsewhere; dopers tended to follow up in everyday life the experiences and insights that came through a high. Consequently, the music that was so wonderful when one was stoned was the music one listened to the rest of the time as well. But beyond that, rock spoke to the realities of life of the era—it spoke "about being yourself, about the terror of [contemporary] life, about the need for love. . . . In listening to such music when high—when the message really gets through—it's more difficult to evade these matters."[13]

✳ ✳ ✳ Rock and Revolution

Underground theorists frequently asserted that rock was revolutionary, although there was no consensus about what that meant. For some, it meant that rock could be used by political revolutionaries in much the same way that country and western music has long been used at political rallies by neopopulists, especially in the South. A few rock bands were avowed revolutionaries; the Detroit group MC5, for example, announced in 1969 that it was "totally committed to the revolution," and its manager, John Sinclair, was given a harsh dope-related prison sentence presumably because of his revolutionary politics. Still, some hippies were skeptics. Ron Jarvis called revolutionary rock "extremely naive and wrong-headed. . . . Music, like the other arts, is anarchic—defying all categories yet paradoxically including them all."[14]

The larger revolutionary role for rock lay outside specifically political arenas; it lay in the purported ability of rock to expose the sham of Western culture and to change the life orientation, political and otherwise, of its listeners. That is the sense in which Jonathan Eisen labeled rock "profoundly subversive."[15] Revolution, that is, could be defined otherwise than as direct political confrontation. Country Joe McDonald noted that "one of the most revolutionary things you can do in this country today is to have a good time and enjoy yourself."[16] Or, as an anonymous writer put it, one shouldn't see "things like music (or whatever) as frivolous to the revolution. Shit, if the revolution is not about our own lives and getting high and smashing the state and getting in touch with ourselves and each other, then it ain't no revolution."[17]

The idea that music has extraordinary potency is hardly a new one. Plato has Socrates remarking to Glaucon in the *Republic* that "musical training is powerful, because rhythm and harmony sink deeply into the soul and fix themselves there solidly."[18] The elder theorist of hip, Ralph Gleason, preached the cultural revolutionary power of rock by quoting the seventeenth-century Scot Andrew Fletcher of Saltoun, "Give me the making of the songs of a nation and I care not who makes its laws."[19] Gleason argued that "Rock music in America has been the single most potent social force for change for several years now,"[20] and "That is why Dylan seems to me to be more important than the Weathermen. They blow buildings in New York. He blew minds all over the world. Ginsberg's poems speak to more people than all the SDS pamphlets put together."[21] As a counterculturist wrote to Abbie Hoffman after he had tried to disrupt the Woodstock festival to make a political point, "Fuck your rhetoric, man . . . it's more fun to dance and sing than fight . . . [and] it's gonna change a lot more heads."[22]

So rock was the revolutionary ultimate. Fundamentalist Christians to the contrary, "WE all know what's going to eventually save the world. Rock, that's what."[23]

But there was always one uncomfortable underside to all that. Rock was inevitably commercialized, partly because the equipment and production expenses for it were high and bills had to be paid. Some hip commentators, therefore, said rock was inherently compromised and couldn't be counted on as the vehicle of the revolution. Common sentiment to the contrary, Irwin Silber argued that the Beatles, Bob Dylan, the Rolling Stones, and even the Fugs were not revolutionaries: "This isn't a put-down, but *revolutionaries do not make it in this system*."[24] But that analysis seemed extreme to most; a middle theoretical ground, therefore, emerged. As Edward Taub put it, "Businessmen can run rock through their $$$ channels, but none can control or regulate the beat, the intangibles which force a person closer to his or her body. Of course, rock 'n' roll won't make the revolution but be it ever so humble, it's playing its role."[25]

✱ ✱ ✱ The Importance of the Lyrics

Although the hippies argued that rock was a totality and that its meaning was not mainly embodied in its lyrics, it is obvious that rock lyrics had a great deal to do with the counterculture's values. They reflected those values, and in turn they helped shape them.

J. L. Simmons and Barry Winograd, in their 1966 survey of the emerging counterculture, detected two essential messages in contemporary rock lyrics: "Come swing with me," an exhortation to drop out of mainstream society (and not so subtly an invitation to sex), and "Myself a stranger in a world I never made," an indictment of majority society and a declaration of alienation.[26] Those kinds of themes arose again and again. Rock lyrics sang the imminent demise of the dominant culture, the urgency of cultural revolution, the dead end of modern technological culture.

Some fairly specific analyses of the content of lyrics were undertaken in hippie days. James T. Carey undertook one of the more detailed studies, analyzing 176 songs (117 of them judged to be rock) popular during a three-month period in 1966. Carey determined that rock supported "new values" (i.e., countercultural values) in 68.1 percent of its lyrics, whereas other forms of music (blues, country, others) supported "old values" (i.e., mainstream values) at an even higher rate, sometimes over 80 percent of the time.[27] At their heart, Carey argued, rock lyrics urged listeners to maximize their freedom in interpersonal relationships and to drop out of conventional society.[28]

Much analysis was applied to the superstars, of course, and preeminently to Bob Dylan. One writer found the heart of Dylan to lie in analyzing America as a speed culture, in perceiving that "most of our technology and institutions are in effect artificial stimulants, which combine to keep us moving faster and faster." In a song like "Desolation Row," Dylan was saying that clear perception, unhindered by speed, is society's desolation row—that is, a place to avoid.[29] A bit more cosmically, Ralph J. Gleason summarized Dylan thus: "He is saying, in short, that the entire system of Western society, built upon Aristotelian logic, the Judeo-Christian ethic and upon a series of economic systems from Hobbes to Marx to Keynes, does not work."[30]

Dylan, though, was notoriously reticent about such analysis. A typical interview:

Q: Your songs are supposed to have a subtle message.
A: Subtle message?
Q: Well, they're supposed to.
A: Where'd you hear that?
Q: In a movie magazine?
A: Oh, —Oh God! Well, we won't—we don't discuss those things here.

Q: Is there anything in addition to your songs that you want to say to people?

A: Good Luck.

Q: You don't say that in your songs.

A: Oh, yes I do, every song tails off with "Good Luck, —I hope you make it."[31]

An interview with John Lennon was only slightly less cryptic:

Q: What about philosophical analyses of your songs?

A: . . . I write lyrics that you don't realize what they mean till after. ESPECIALLY some of the better songs or some of the more flowing ones, like "Walrus." The whole first verse was written without any knowledge. And "Tomorrow Never Knows"—I didn't know what I was saying, and you just find out later, that's why these people are good on them.

Q: Pop analysts are often trying to read something into songs that isn't there.

A: It is there. It's like abstract art really. It's just the same really. It's just that when you have to think about it to write it, it just means that you labored at it. But when you *say* it, man, you know you're saying it, it's a continuous flow.

Q: [lines from "Penny Lane":] A pretty nurse is selling poppies from a tray/ And though she thinks she's in a play/ She is anyway.

A: It's always been a bit of "She's in a play, she is anyway heh heh" because you're saying that again and again, it's a game, man, it's a game, but because you mean it, it's all right, it's ok.[32]

Finally, meaning came when the song interacted with the listener. "Lucy in the Sky with Diamonds" was one of the most celebrated acid songs ever, what with its titular acronym, but the Beatles consistently maintained that the acronym was purely accidental: "We didn't notice it said 'LSD' until somebody told us. Everybody interprets things in his own way."[33]

✳ ✳ ✳ Rock Capitalism

Given the inescapable relation of rock to technology and
therefore to money, capitalists popped up to profit from the sound.
Most hippies resented rock capitalism, at least when it was undertaken
by persons whose hearts were not hip.

Commercialization of music was nothing new in counterculture
days, but it did represent a special problem for a movement not fond
of capitalism and in any event devoted to seek its meaning outside the
courts of the establishment. John Landau observed in *Rolling Stone*,
itself a piece of rock-based capitalism, "Rock, the music of the Sixties, was a music of spontaneity. . . . As that spontaneity and creativity
have become more stylized and analyzed and structured, it has become easier for businessmen and behind-the-scenes manipulators to
structure their approach to merchandising music." [34]

Capitalists ended up making more from the music than hippie musicians did, and the best artists inevitably became capitalists. But it wasn't
just a matter of having cynical materialists cash in on hip music; the
financial structure of things affected the music itself, commercializing
rock as it looked for "short-term profit and premature hardening of
the categories" which was "in almost dialectical opposition to the leading principles of this cultural revolution" which stood for "communalism, participation, and, where possible, joy." [35]

Thus was the dilemma posed, and the counterculture never solved
it—indeed could not have solved it, given the hippies' disdain for
analysis and planning. The music was too important to boycott; there
were a few vague calls for communal alternatives to concerts and
records, but never any workable programs. [36]

Perhaps the closest thing to a hip type of rock capitalism was the
bootleg-record industry, which made unauthorized recordings of live
concerts and distributed copies of illicitly acquired unreleased commercial tapes. But the bootleggers had bills to pay and thus became
underground capitalists themselves; moreover, their products tended
to be expensive and their quality low. Ultimately, therefore, the music
that was the language of a generation was controlled by the interests it
was supposed to be overthrowing. Period.

✻ ✻ ✻ Festivals and Concerts as Sacramental Gatherings

The great rock festivals and concerts were the definitive gatherings of the countercultural faithful. They were as important to the hip world as any pilgrimages, crusades, or revivals have ever been to their own milieux. They helped shape rock and provided the best opportunities for massive indulgence in the sacraments: dope, nudity, sex, rock, community.

The lesser services were the ballroom concerts, which occurred in cities everywhere. In the right setting, a concert could be an enormous turn-on: "Call it salvation through Hard Rock," one hipster wrote. "Through total sensory involvement, the mind is to be freed."[37] Indeed, so important did the ballroom concerts become that the names of the biggest halls took on a mythic aura: Fillmore, East and West; Winterland; the Avalon.

But the ultimate experience came at the great outdoor festivals, which ironically charted their own demise, since their immense size and freewheeling nature (laws can't be enforced when there are 100,000 criminals present) led to enormous public resistance to their existence. The chemistry of the festivals was complex. Music was the main attraction, nominally; but the real point was the community offstage. There was a sense of cultural identity at the festivals that simply could not be found elsewhere. The individual faded; the crowd became an organism, "something alive of itself."[38] There was nothing more entirely hip than the festivals.

The two giant festivals of 1969 displayed the full spectrum of the potential and problems of the genre. Woodstock, in August, drew unfavorable comments at first in the public press, since it happened in the rain and suffered major breakdowns of support facilities. But it was quickly mythologized by the counterculture as the epitome of joy and peace.[39] Woodstock was to the hippies all and everything: a cataclysm, a political event, a religious experience, a glimpse of communism, the pinnacle of passive consumerism, and the first free dope territory in America.[40] A few days after it was over, one participant proclaimed that "the historians will have to reckon with it . . . these young revolutionaries are on their way . . . to slough away the life-style that isn't theirs . . . and find one that is."[41] Woodstock was "a confused, chaotic founding of something new, something our world must now find a way to deal with. The limits have changed now, they've been pushed out, the priorities have been re-arranged, and new, 'impractical' ideas must be taken seriously. The mind boggles."[42]

Woodstock was an obvious disaster: the sanitary, food, and medical facilities were overwhelmed and broke down while rain turned Max Yasgur's meadow into a quagmire. But all that simply made things cohere. "When a natural disaster strikes, people pull together in a rare way that they all remember with amazement years later," a Liberation News Service release announced a few days afterwards.[43] Or, as Wavy Gravy (Hugh Romney) said from the stage at the concert, "There's always a little bit of heaven in a disaster area." The physical conditions were bad, and Woodstock was after all a commercial enterprise operated for profit—but that didn't dampen the reality of the festival as a vision of a new reality. "Woodstock must always be [our] model of how good we will all feel after the revolution," Andrew Kopkind wrote, summing up the consensus.[44] As it turned out, it was never quite to happen again. But the dream had been dreamed and was not easily stilled:

> Maybe, just maybe, it will be a new beginning for us despite our walking away from the most beautiful experience many ever had. . . . We now know we can live together as we had only done previously in our fantasies. No one will leave here the same person that existed before. For a few days we were all in a beautiful place. Can we do it again? All I know is I don't want to leave here. I feel like I've come home.[45]

If Woodstock was a glimpse of the best the future could hold, the Rolling Stones concert at Altamont, California, a few weeks later provided a refresher course in grim reality. As the Berkeley *Barb* recorded it,

> Someone was knifed to death. Lots of people were beaten. Love and peace were fucked by the Hell's Angels in front of hundreds of thousands of people who did nothing. The brothers and sisters . . . could have cooled the Angels and any other violence spuming toughs, but they just let hate happen.[46]

What went wrong? Mismanagement, perhaps; rumor had it that the Hell's Angels were hired as security guards and were paid in advance with a truckload of beer. Or perhaps heaven can be achieved only once. Whatever the case, soon after Woodstock peace and joy had given way to ugliness. Some went so far as to say that the concert marked the end of hip.[47] Few were as optimistic as Timothy Leary:

> One thing that has to be said about Altamont is that there were three or four hundred thousand people there who did sit peaceably and get high and watch the sun and the clouds and the stars and listen to the music and were not at all involved in the violence. . . . There were less than fifty violent people there in a throng of 400,000. In a sense Altamont is a Microcosm of the overall political situation. 99 percent of everybody wants to get high, and groove and love. . . .[48]

Some could even dismiss the murder: "Four babies are born and four people die. An even exchange of souls."[49] In any event, most remembered that the festivals on the whole were overwhelmingly positive events. Good reports continued to filter in from festivals in the years following Woodstock and Altamont. Thus festivals were mythologized as high-water marks of the counterculture, giving those attending— and even those just dreaming of attending—a taste of Nirvana.

The communal bus of Ken Kesey and the Merry Pranksters heralded the arrival of the hippie era. (Copyright © Gene Anthony 1980)

The Charlatans, the original hip rock and roll band, were star performers during the Summer of Love (1967) in San Francisco. (Copyright © Gene Anthony 1980)

Anonymous cartoon.

American culture was at a dead end, the hippies argued. (Copyright © R. Crumb 1990. Used with permission of Last Gasp of San Francisco)

The New Left and the hippies were often at odds, but they had much in common. John Sinclair, manager of the rock group MC5, and his office illustrate the overlap. (John and Leni Sinclair Collection, Michigan Historical Collection, Bentley Historical Library, University of Michigan)

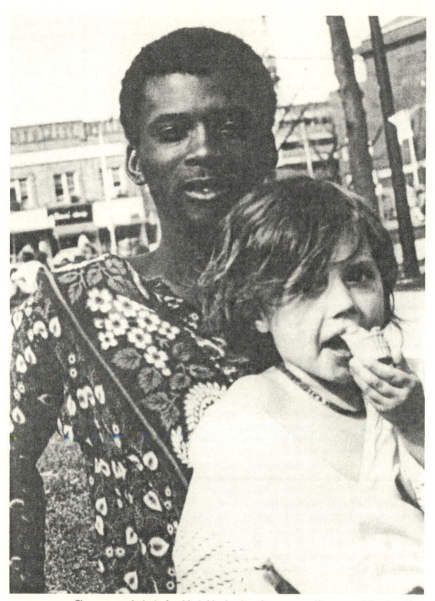

There were relatively few black hippies, but they were readily accepted by the white majority. (John and Leni Sinclair Collection, Michigan Historical Collection, Bentley Historical Library, University of Michigan)

WANTED

Jesus Christ

WANTED FOR SEDITION, CRIMINAL
ANARCHY, VAGRANCY, AND CONSPIR-
ING TO OVERTHORW THE ESTABLISHED
GOVERNMENT.

Dresses Poorly. Said To Be A Carpenter
By Trade, Ill-nourished, Has Visionary
Ideas, Associates With Common Working
People, The Unemployed And Bums.

Alien—Believed to be a Jew

Alias— 'Prince of Peace' King of the Jews'
'Son of Man' Light of the World', etc., etc.

Professional Agitator

Red Beard, marks on Hands and Feet—
The Result of Injuries Inflicted By an
Angry Mob Led By Respectable Citizens
and Legal Authorities.

The hippies admired a radical Jesus but not the churches that operated in his name.

What could be finer than a healthy stand of marijuana? (John and Leni Sinclair Collection, Michigan Historical Collection, Bentley Historical Library, University of Michigan)

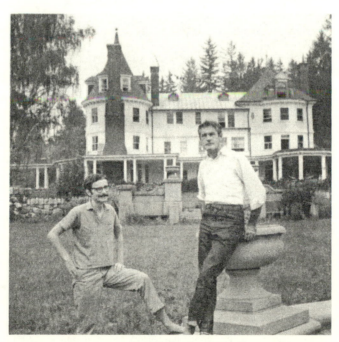

As faculty members at Harvard, Ralph Metzner and Timothy Leary were early prophets of LSD. Later they took up residence at Millbrook, an estate owned by the wealthy family of some of their followers. (*New York Daily News*)

What the country needed most was dope, the hippies believed. (Copyright ©
R. Crumb 1990). Used with permission of Last Gasp of San Francisco)

Beware! **Young and Old — People in All Walks of Life!**

Marihuana Cigarette

This **may be handed you**

by the friendly stranger. It contains the Killer Drug "Marihuana"-- a powerful narcotic in which lurks

Murder! Insanity! Death!

WARNING!

Dope peddlers are shrewd! They may put some of this drug in the ☕ or in the ᴄᴏᴄᴋ ᴛᴀɪʟ or in the tobacco cigarette.

WRITE FOR DETAILED INFORMATION, ENCLOSING 12 CENTS IN POSTAGE — MAILING COST

Address: THE INTER-STATE NARCOTIC ASSOCIATION

Old anti-marijuana posters were reprinted and became popular satiric artifacts in hip culture. (Kansas collection, University of Kansas Libraries)

Body paint, beads, and advocacy of the use of LSD were all thoroughly hip.

LSD was the answer to everything. (Kansas Collection, University of Kansas Libraries)

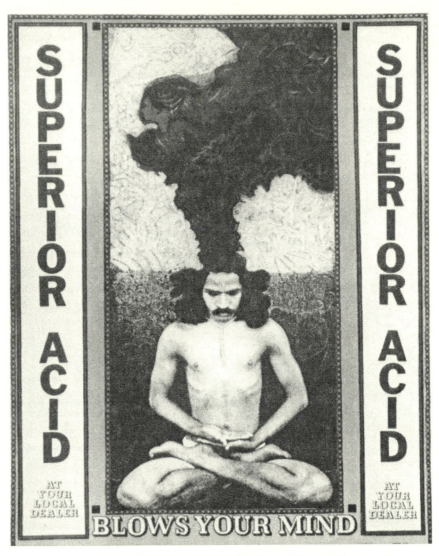

Many countercultural posters glorified LSD. (Kansas Collection, University of Kansas Libraries)

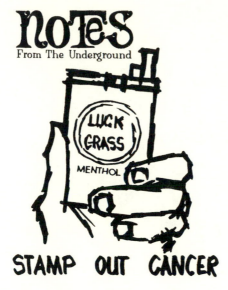

NOTES
From The Underground

STAMP OUT CANCER

Hippies believed marijuana to be much healthier than tobacco.

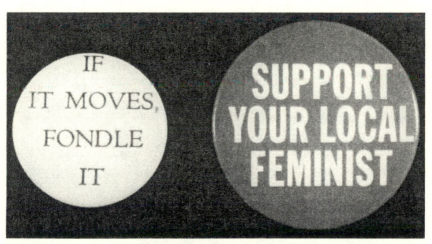

Two hippie buttons expressed rather contradictory ideas about sexual politics.

WOMEN'S SOLIDARITY STRIKE

Militant feminism became increasingly prevalent in the very late 1960s and early 1970s.

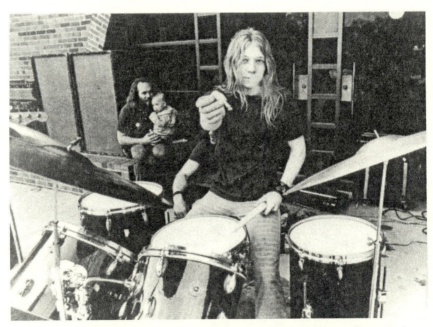

Rock musicians were important participants in the dope subculture. (John and Leni Sinclair Collection, Michigan Historical Collection, Bentley Historical Library, University of Michigan)

An early poster promoting a new San Francisco band called the Jefferson Airplane. (Kansas Collection, University of Kansas Libraries)

The Mothers of Invention was one of the more unorthodox hippie bands. (Kansas Collection, University of Kansas Libraries)

Domes made of automobile tops dominated the architecture of Drop City, near
Trinidad, Colorado. (Gene and Jo Ann Bernofsky)

Drop City. (Gene and Jo Ann Bernofsky)

The first Be-In (San Francisco, January 1967) saw an outpouring of counterculture peace and love. (Copyright © Gene Anthony 1990)

Organized love: the Diggers of San Francisco and elsewhere fed and clothed many destitute hippies. (Copyright © Gene Anthony 1990)

Hippie politics emphasized love, not violence.

The hippie love of nature and desire for a cleaner environment led many to try to eat healthier food. (John and Leni Sinclair Collection, Michigan Historical Collection, Bentley Historical Library, University of Michigan)

Rationality was disdained by the hippies. (Copyright © R. Crumb 1990. Used with permission of Last Gasp of San Francisco)

A few of the thousands of children born at The Farm, an ongoing hippie commune in Tennessee. (Photo by Albert Bates © 1990 The Second Foundation. Reprinted by permission)

I AM
CURED, I'M
NOT A HIPPIE
ANYMORE

CHAPTER 5

The Ethics of Community

Now you see. This is it—you only have to come here to realize it. That's why we haven't been hassled. All the county officials and inspectors who come here realize that this is a better way of life than theirs. They know this is the answer just as you do.

—Olompali commune member, Berkeley *Barb*, 12–18 July 1968

Intentional community is a vision that has a long and honorable history in human culture. The Buddhist *sangha*, or monastic order, is alive and well after some 2,500 years, making it surely the oldest human institution. The early Christians practiced community of goods. In America, the original Native-American settlers lived communally, and some of the later settlers established utopian settlements as well. Thus the communes of the hippies represented an old ideal— presented in new garb.

The hippies, for their part, were not usually students of communal history, and in any event they tended to believe, as one of them put it, that "the hippie development is of a totally new order, wherein the past, in a sense, is irrelevant."[1] For one thing, most earlier communes were based on either religious or radical political conviction and thus had a clear ideological center and strong sense of purpose. The hip communes, on the other hand, tended toward free expression, hedonism, and anarchy, and they represented an attempt to live the hippie ethical ideals of liberated sex, use of dope, love, and sharing. Although few of them lasted more than a year or two, they attracted uncounted thousands of residents and even more sympathetic visitors. A few of them have survived, some of them now closing in on the quarter-century of longevity which makes them "successful" in Rosabeth Moss Kanter's widely accepted analysis,[2] and they represent one of the most tangible remaining links with hip culture.

Several have tried to estimate the size of the hippie communal movement. Jules Siegel, writing in 1970, quoted a *Newsweek* estimate of 500 communes with ten thousand members in 1969, and a listing of 120 active communes in *The Modern Utopian*.[3] Benjamin Zablocki estimated in 1971 that there were then some 1,000 rural countercultural communes and about 200 urban communes.[4] Keith Melville, in 1972, similarly estimated the number of communes as "at least a thousand."[5] And beyond those who actually lived in communes, thousands more who were, for whatever reason, unable to live in them admired the whole effort from afar. The ideal of community, in short, was powerful in the counterculture.

Communalism was present from the earliest days of the counter culture. Tolstoy Farm, founded in Washington State in 1963, was probably the first commune with a hip spirit. Two years later, a more thoroughly hip commune, Drop City, was founded outside Trinidad, Colorado. Originally established as an artists' community, its striking domes covered with automobile tops became a prominent landmark in the hip communal scene, and it lasted through the heyday of the counterculture. Another early entrant was the anarchical Morning Star Ranch outside Sebastopol, California. The mushrooming of communes after Morning Star, however, was widely believed in hippiedom to be related to the proliferation of rock festivals. The festivals were short-lived communes of a sort, as indeed were other music festivals before them. David Satterfield put it this way:

> Communalism and participation, both, are best synthesized on a musical level in traditional festivals like the old-time fiddlers' conventions. But the interaction of different social classes is more advanced in Bluegrass festivals, where dancing gives way to actually picking music together.[6]

So the rock festivals took an existing phenomenon to a new level of intensity; festival participants repeatedly emphasized an overwhelming sense of community that provided an impulse for continuing communal experimentation. The definitive festival in this regard was, of course, Woodstock, which was held in 1969. Reports on Woodstock in the underground press repeatedly stressed the feeling of unity: "Everyone needed other people's help, and everyone was ready to share what he had as many ways as it could be split up. Everyone could feel the good vibrations. . . ."[7] And from that feeling came the vision that free people could create "instant communities" where they could "live on their own terms."[8] The Hog Farm commune of New Mexico was influential at Woodstock; it was a working commune that provided support facilities (food, medicine, crisis intervention) for the festival. Although many communes predated Woodstock, that festival became the symbol of a new cultural reality in which the call to community was compelling.

But rock did not contribute to communalism only at the point of the festival. The music itself was believed to feed the communal impulse:

> The rock experience at its most intense is an imitation of engulfment and merger, a route to a flowing, ego-transcending oneness. As fans and enemies alike know, rock sound overwhelms separateness, the mental operations that discern and define here and there, me and not me. . . . Pounded by volume, riddled by light, the listener slides free from the restraining self and from the pretenses of a private "unique" rationality.[9]

Moreover, many rock bands themselves were models of communal living centered on a specific purpose.[10] One writer called them "superfamilies," "far more intimately interrelated and integrated than any corporate ensembles in the past"; indeed, rock itself was a "tribal phenomenon, immune to definition."[11] The band members were idealized as like unto the troubadours of old, singing and playing "to make people happy and to keep food in their mouths."[12]

So rock was seen as an essential in the rise of communalism. It helped people realize, as Tuli Kupferberg put it, that "Two can live more better (as we used to say at P.S. 82) than one. So can three or four (or any number?)."[13] And the ultimate vision was one of cosmic-level communalism:

> We are moving towards a conscious community of artists and lovers who live together, work together, share all things—smoke dope together, dance and fuck together, and spread the word together every way we can—through our dress, our freedom of

movement, our music and dance, our economy, our human social forms, through our every breath on this planet.[14]

Dope, it should be noted, played its own role in the rise of communalism. Dope engendered a sort of community of its own in the sense that lawbreakers have something important in common, and that if they stick together they will probably improve their chances of staying out of jail. Rural communes might be isolated enough that the use of dope would be relatively harder for the authorities to detect, and it is fair to surmise that the search for inconspicuous places to grow marijuana moved more than one hippie to move to a rural commune.

Beyond that, dope was believed to spread the communal spirit. As Stanley Krippner and Don Fersh noted, dope tended "to weaken ego boundaries, leading an individual to conclude that 'we are all one.'"[15]

✳ ✳ ✳ Community as an Ideal

Countercultural communes were means rather than ends. The end was affinity, communication, humans caring for each other, a new way of living; the communes were, in the words of one hip writer, "a means, a way, to bring us and our people closer together—closer to social freedom."[16] As another put it, "The commune itself is not an end product or a beginning. It's only an experience where we can learn to communicate in this way."[17]

And then, suddenly it hits you like a ton of bricks. These hippies, these rebels, these dropouts, left to their own devices, what have they done? What new and dangerous things have they done? Why, they have fashioned a life composed of community, hard work, the family, religion. They have re-created (in their own image, to be sure) an old knowledge fired by a new passion, born of original discovery. They have given new life to old, old needs. Because what they want, in a word, is only a real life. Not a novel life. Not an aboriginal, orgiastic fantasy of a life. Only a *real* life.

The urgency of this need, and only the urgency of this need, accounts for the continued existence of the communes.[18]

The new life being pursued by the communards was a deliberate repudiation of majority society; the communes were a major vehicle for dropping out of the old and into the new. As religious studies scholar William C. Shepherd observed,

> In counter culture religiosity there is not so much a balanced dialectic between communitas and society, but instead an emphatic insistence that the communitas is the real thing, that one in fact need not reenter the ordinary world, that one can somehow abnegate its rules altogether not just momentarily.[19]

That feeling of dropping out and building anew gave communes much of whatever strength they had. It provided a sort of emotional solidarity in a commune which, as Ed Schwartz put it, does not come from physical closeness itself, as any subway rider knows.[20]

The precise content of this solidarity defies exact definition, however. Robert Houriet, an early and perceptive observer of hip communes, asserted that it could not be understood with analytical tools, since the communes depended on a totally different consciousness than the straight world had, one that would not separate person and nature, self and society.[21] The trappings of communes, such as leftist ideology, communist economics, sexual freedom, and so forth, all faded before this fundamental consciousness. The goal was to become one in the New Age, to submerge the ego into the common mind and heart. Persons kept their abilities and needs, but the goal was to integrate those abilities and needs with the good of the community.

✱ ✱ ✱ The Rural Impulse

The counterculture grew up largely in cities and its participants came primarily from metropolitan areas, so it is of interest to note that hippie communes were ideally located in the country.[22] According to the counterculture, not only were cities physically intolerable for life ("Just name me one person who could live there without some kind of mind-fucking Forget pill ingested daily, or seven times daily, pills and smokes, tokes and needles, tabs and hits."[23]); they were also incompatible with a liberated or tribal lifestyle. The only places where urban hip living was possible, according to Raymond Mungo, were those in which the counterculture was so populous as to make good commercial sense to capitalists.[24] "Yes—brotherhood cannot develop inside the city. . . . Grab a car, some acid, (and of course man's staple—marijuana) and head for the ocean (or the woods, or actually anyway towards a decentralized humanoid existence)."[25] Those in cities became infected with classic rural romanticism: an "army of peaceful guerillas [is] ready to turn [its] back on the already ravaged cities and the inoperable 'life-styles,' imminently prepared to move onto the mist-covered fields and into the cool, still woods."[26] The appeal was powerful and mystical. Timothy Leary put it succinctly: "The key issue . . . is LAND."[27]

But a real-world problem immediately presented itself: where does a group of voluntarily poor young persons find land to live on? Buying land required more capital than was available to the typical hippie, to say the least. Buying land, anyway, seemed a wrong beginning, as Raymond Mungo noted: "It is a foolish notion, this land ownership; and men are made fools by it. . . . If you belong to the land, you'll stay there; but if the land belongs to you, you'll lose it for sure, in some way."[28]

Accordingly some had visions of free land, land opened to all comers by those fortunate enough to be able to own it. The archetypal experiment of that type was conducted by the musician Lou Gottlieb, who opened his Morning Star Ranch without restriction. Gottlieb naively claimed that his plan couldn't fail, simply because the sort of person who would be attracted to such a concept would be one with a high capacity for community and toleration of others. But in practice, Morning Star lurched between the Scylla of residents incapable of the sharing and constructive giving necessary to make the community work and the Charybdis of continued confrontations with public officials determined to police such things as sanitation, minimum housing standards, and lawlessness.[29]

Another solution to the problem of providing land for those who would live on it was the proposed Earth People's Park. The idea took shape in the wake of Woodstock; the original plan involved the purchase of a huge tract of land (perhaps five thousand acres or more, probably in New Mexico) with money raised from a huge rock concert on the land itself.[30] Later a decentralized version of the plan emerged, one which would have had many smaller parks. The Hog Farm rolling commune toured the country for a time trying to raise seed money and make arrangements for the plan, but its logistical problems were overwhelming and compounded by the fact that in few proposed locations did the locals relish the notion of an invasion of zillions of hippies. After some months of earnest effort the plan crumbled.

The rural impulse was a part of the hippie preference for the natural over the artificial, the organic over the plastic. In the country, a clan could grow and consume its own food free of contaminants, breathe clean air, be naked at will, be close to nature and to the cosmic forces. Getting clean and pure and back to basics was a major part of the communal equation.

✳ ✳ ✳ New Family Structures

Part of the communal push was a new sense of family structure. For the hippies, the biological family gave way to the cultural tribe. Kinship and relationships were up for grabs. Allen Ginsberg, for example, saw a host of new possibilities:

We obviously are changing, altering in family structure. . . . There's no reason to think it so strange that it might alter in a direction that some groups of people might want. And the tendency toward a commune and community and enlarged family is a very definite tendency. . . . I would see different kinds of family structure. Couple of girls with one guy, couple of guys with one girl, 20 girls, 20 guys, all making it if they want. Children held in common, matrilineal descent . . . sharing.[31]

Timothy Leary identified the new family concept as making the difference between survival and failure of groups within the counterculture. Many "were not able to defend themselves because they didn't have any solid spiritual core, any rooted family centeredness."[32] A new type of close-knit family was the goal, and communalism could help the hippies get there.

✳ ✳ ✳ Varieties of Communes

The predominant public image of the hippie commune was of a rundown farm in some backwoods location, but in reality there was quite a diversity to the communal scene. There were urban and rural, drug-using and drug-free, egalitarian and chauvinistic, structured and anarchical, religious and secular communes, to name just a few of the antitypes.

Quite a few hip authors constructed typologies of communes. Ed Schwartz, for example, categorized them by purpose and came up with four types:

1. Therapeutic communes were those formed for the working out of the common psychological problems or social situations of the persons involved, as in the case of women wrestling with sexism or young runaways trying to cope with their problems.
2. Fraternal communes were made up of lonely individuals who simply wanted to live with others.
3. Utopian communes were formed to demonstrate to the world a new way of living, to prove the superiority of the hip way of life. These groups were probably the ones that received the most public attention but were not necessarily the most common.
4. Organizing communes were those with a common ideology, program, or strategy for social change. Such communes were united largely by their participants' opposition to the prevailing sociopolitical system and, in some cases, by their sharing of the risks of radical dissent.[33]

Schwartz missed one important countercultural communal type, the religious. New religions were part of the countercultural matrix, and several of them operated communes for some or all of their members. The Hare Krishna movement, founded in the United States in 1965 and intimately related to the hippies in its early years, was largely communal. The Jesus freaks who appeared in the latter days of hip founded an extensive network of communes. And independent spiritual communes were also founded in considerable numbers. Many of the religious communes were not exactly fully countercultural, however, even though they drew their members from the ranks of the hippies, used the hip argot, and shared with the hippies an anti-Establishment outlook. The Hare Krishnas, to cite an extreme example, rejected all intoxicants, nearly all sex, rock and roll and other Western music, and all kinds of activities not deemed properly transcendental. Boundary lines between hip and straight were always impossible to draw precisely, and the religious communes had feet in more than one world.

Another typology of communes was based upon the structures and organizational patterns that the groups took. One such scheme was proposed by Stanley Krippner and Don Fersh on the basis of their observation of eighteen major communes. They ended up with three types of communities: (1) "The secular commune which is relatively unstructured and which functions with a minimum of administration" (the freewheeling Morning Star in California would again be a good example); (2) "The secular commune which is relatively structured and which operates within an administrative framework," one which often functioned because of the presence of a strong leader; and (3) "The structured, highly-organized religious commune," such as New Vrindaban, the Hare Krishna communal farm in West Virginia, or the less sectarian but still spiritually oriented Lama Foundation at San Cristobal, New Mexico.[34]

Many other typologies of communes could be constructed. The point is that communalism in the counterculture was ideologically, organizationally, and spiritually diverse.

On the other hand, there were also some fairly broad similarities among the communes. Most of them professed to reject materialism in favor of spiritual growth, however defined. They were committed to toleration, attracting and usually coping with a wide variety of members. They were bastions of the culture of opposition; by definition, the communards were committed to dropping out of majority society. Finally, many commune residents tended to be inwardly oriented, wanting to live freely without interfering or being interfered with by the outside world any more than was necessary.

✳ ✳ ✳ Drawbacks and Problems with Communes

As beatific as the communal vision was, reality was something else. No hip commune avoided a host of problems, and in many cases the problems rose up to drown the commune. There are no reliable statistics on the fluid communal movement of the counterculture, but average longevity could not have been high.

One common problem in communes was that these "liberated" utopias all too often were not at all enlightened about women. Many hip women found communal life oppressive, and more than a few were led to the then-emerging women's movement, both by their treatment at the hands of certain communal men and by the feminist solidarity that often developed among women at a commune. Kit Leder, reflecting on life in a twelve-member farm commune in the summer of 1969, wrote afterwards:

> Even though there was no society-dictated division of labor, even though we had complete freedom to determine the division of labor for ourselves, a well-known pattern emerged immediately. Women did most of the cooking, all of the cleaning up, and, of course, the washing. They also worked in the fields all day—so that after the farm work was finished, the men could be found sitting around talking and taking naps while the women prepared supper. In addition to that, one of the women remained in camp every day in order to cook lunch—it was always a woman who did this, never a man. Of course, the women were excused from some of the tasks; for example, none of us ever drove a tractor. That was considered too complicated for a woman.[35]

Building on that analysis, Vivian Estellachild wrote of her experience living in two communes:

> Although communal living appears to be a step in the right direction, the hip commune uses women in a group way the same as the fathers did in a one-to-one way. The communes are too fluid to create any security for a woman. Her stability lost and isolation complete, she cannot be an effective force for change.
> The source of our oppression is *all men*, no exceptions for bells and beads.[36]

But it needs to be said as well that not all situations were oppressive. About the same time that Leder and Estellachild were finding communal life a dead-end for women, Marilyn Foster was having an opposite experience in a Baltimore commune:

> The men and women in Toad Hall have enabled each other to move outside of male-female roles and expectations. . . . Our community arrangement offers the support and acceptance necessary in a society which alienates us from who we are and where we want to go. We don't have all the answers—but we are picking up some good leads.[37]

Women's issues were not the only problems with communes. Indeed, difficulties were rife; the typical lifespan of a hippie commune was not long. Ed Schwartz, in his discussion of communal problems, concluded that three general problems underlay communal failure: (1) members joined for very different personal reasons, and thus the group lacked coherent direction; (2) many communes failed to enforce agreements or rules, since an authoritarian structure tended to be suspect in the counterculture; and (3) many communes were incapable of changing communal goals in response to new situations and insights. The fundamental problem, wrote Schwartz, was that for most people God was dead, and therefore there was no belief or ideology strong enough to sustain any but the most intensely religious communes.[38]

Certainly a major underlying source of communal problems was the fact that in many cases communes proved attractive to individuals whose interest in new ways of living was related to their failure to function effectively in conventional society—that is, persons whose basic nature or personal problems made them terrible candidates for group living. Keith Melville quoted Horace Greeley—himself a vocal supporter of communalism in the nineteenth century—to that effect:

> A serious obstacle to the success of any socialistic experiment must always be confronted. I allude to the kind of persons who are naturally attracted to it. Along with many noble and lofty souls, whose impulses are purely philanthropic, and who are willing to labor and suffer reproach for any cause that promises to benefit mankind, there throng scores of whom the world is quite worthy—the conceited, played-out, the idle, and the good-for-nothing generally; who, finding themselves utterly out of place and at a dis-

count in the world as it is, rashly conclude that they are exactly fitted for the world as it ought to be.[39]

So, in reality, many of the communes attracted more than their share of deadbeats, drunks, drug (as opposed to dope) users, abusers of women, and other undesirables. Communities with open-door policies —initially there were many of them—naturally suffered more from the problem than the more selective ones did. In any event, personnel problems had more than a little to do with the fact that most communes, and especially the anarchistic ones, were short lived. A few with some kind of vision or unusually competent leadership survived; some are still alive at this writing, many of them healthier than ever.

Whatever the stories of success or failure of specific communes, the counterculture retained its dedication to the ideal of community. Though some communes did not last long, the general feeling (or rationalization) was that "all of the communities were successful for what was learned in them."[40]

Community is neither more nor less than a mutual commitment to share in the pursuit of a common vision; and given the conditions of the day, one would hope that it be the vision of justice for all. If the communes can generate this vision, if they can nurture and sustain it, then all power to them. If not, then all the power in the world will not rescue them from the morass in which they currently find themselves.[41]

✳ ✳ ✳ A Note on Individualism and Collectivism

On several occasions, observers of the counterculture criticized the hippies for being conformists in a movement that supposedly rejected conformism, for being obedient sheep instead of the individualists they claimed to be. Wrote one doctor sympathetic to the counterculture, "I'm concerned with the great deal of group conformity that exists in the hip movement. It's supposed to be the antithesis of conformity."[42] Others noted at least an ambivalence on the question, since the counterculture embraced communes along with anarchy and free self-expression.[43]

For the hippies themselves, that criticism was misdirected. The world of hip never idealized individualism; after all, "individualism" of a particularly constrained type (the type more accurately labeled "self-ishness") was one of the central cancers of Establishment society. It led people to be indifferent or antagonistic toward others; it moved people toward unconcern about the environment; it made social problems fester. Although the hippies were colorful, even flamboyant, in their rejection of majority society, individualism was not any kind of ultimate concern for them. As a hip writer wrote in an Atlanta underground paper, "Instead of millions of young individuals, what we now have is an entire generation moving headlong into a collective consciousness."[44]

Criticism of American individualism was a staple topic for hip-oriented writers. "Individualism," wrote Philip Slater, "is a kind of desperate plea to save all mutants, on the grounds that we do not know what we are or what we need." Loss of individualism "in some degree, is just the price we must pay for a tolerable life in a tolerable community."[45] To the counterculture, the fruits of individualism were privatism, competition, elitism, selfishness, jealousy, and reinforcement of the territorial imperative, all of which were evil. "Generally we were raised in a world where survival was strictly for self, for self gain, for self survival. . . . Now the pendulum is coming to a point where the only way we will survive is when everybody is doing for each other."[46]

Slater described this excessive individualism as being uniquely related to American culture. America, he wrote, provides one of the few societies in which the welfare of the individual has not been subordinated to that of the group. "Americans are forced into making more choices per day, with fewer givens, more ambiguous criteria, less environmental stability, and less social structural support, than any people in history." Thus it is that the three "human desires" of community, engagement, and dependence have been "deeply and uniquely frustrated by American culture."[47]

Therefore, the counterculture opted for collectivism. In the realms of both possessions and the self, self-denial for the community was the order of the day. At Woodstock, "although local residents were reported to be demanding 25 cents for a glass of water and $1 for a loaf of bread and a quart of milk, on the festival grounds, sharing what you had—whether a bonfire, an apple or a joint—was the order of the night."[48] Throughout the counterculture, the price of admission was "the sacrifice of one's individual pride, no one can do it by themselves, that's the trip back into the dark ages."[49] One learned

> that one restricts one's freedom in order to taste the sweetness of freedom earned, freedom defined, freedom marked off; that one gains the whole of oneself by giving up a part of oneself; that [people], in order to call themselves anything, must call themselves members of a nation.[50]

So far from individualism was the counterculture that the exercise of the ego itself was regarded as needing tight limits. Mungo wrote that countercultural life required "a death of the ego";[51] Paul Goodman wrote that the original sin was to be on an ego trip that isolated one from the community.[52] In the place of individuals, the community itself became the basic reality.

Certainly the retreat from individualism was, as so many other things in the counterculture were, related to dope. Psychedelic experience was not just something internal and private for the individual; it was an article of faith that the expansion of mind helped one forgo the ego and learn that there was "one transient energy process hooked with the energy dance about him."[53]

And once the collective consciousness had been realized on that level, the way was opened for an individualism of sorts that was far better than the law of the jungle. It was an individualism that did not reduce self to selfishness, one that let each person have a sphere of operation within the community, one that allowed for an innocent, free flowering of personality compatible with the needs of the people united. It is in that spirit that the countercultural aphorism "Do your own thing" should be understood. Flamboyant self-expression was wonderful—but one's first commitment had to be to the group, not the self.

CHAPTER 6

The Ethics of Cultural Opposition

REMEMBER: The *first* revolution (but not of course the last) is in yr own head.

Dump out *their* irrational goals, desires, morality.

—Tuli Kupferberg, in Joseph Berke, *Counter Culture*, 1969, p. 85.

The idea is that we have no ideas. We want to abolish ideas. What we want is peace, communication, and escape from automation.

—"Anthony," *Florida Free Press*, 30 June 1968

The counterculture never saw itself as just another subculture; it was the Disloyal Opposition to Establishment culture. And from the beginning, cultural conflict was the order of the day—if only, as the hippies saw It, because the majoritarians insisted on confrontation with the hippies, arresting them for sale and possession of dope and trying to block rock festivals and communes. Thus, the culture of peace and love was also a culture of confrontation and conflict.

The major themes of the culture of opposition—dope, sex, rock and roll, and community—have been the topics of the preceding chapters of this book. The more optimistic of the hippies, however, had a vision of creating a whole new culture, and the new ethics they proposed touched nearly all parts of life. This chapter provides an overview of several other important themes in hip ethics, demonstrating the breadth of the hippie critique and, thereby, the depth of the discontent and alienation the hippies felt from the dominant culture.

One need not read very far in countercultural literature to realize the centrality of its contention that American culture had, by mid-century, reached a dead end. The stranglehold of technocrats, bigots, and incompetents on American institutions had reached the point, the hippies believed, that an even moderately sensitive person had to cry "Enough! There has to be something better than all of this!"

Cultural opposition was not, however, merely a naysaying. Although hipness was a rebellion, it was a rebellion with a vision, a sort of insurrectionary artist's eye. The hippies offered broad goals for a humane society: creativity, decentralization, distrust of bureaucratic and hierarchical structures, freedom, pleasure, anti-authoritarianism, direct and honest contact among persons, and the discarding of restrictions and inhibitions. Examining a variety of such themes is the job of this chapter.

✳ ✳ ✳ Love Is All You Need

Nothing more identified the counterculture in its early days than "peace and love." The hippies constituted the love generation, a people of peace, sweetness, flowers, light, optimism. The epitome of the spirit of love came with the great Be-Ins (unstructured massive gatherings of the countercultural faithful). At the first of these, at Golden Gate Park in San Francisco on 14 January 1967, it was reported that there was "no anger, no reproach for the act of non-love. . . . Some say as many as [twenty thousand] were present and all seemed filled, contented and giving."[1] *Love* was one of the most frequently used words in the hippie vocabulary, and even the editors of *Time* concluded, in their 1967 cover story on the hippies, that "The key ethical element in the hippie movement is love—indiscriminate and all-embracing, fluid and changeable, directed at friend and foe alike."[2]

Love is a word with a variety of definitions, and it meant several things to the counterculture. In its most simple and direct sense, love was an emotion, a state of mind, a feeling that radiated optimistic moral power. Hippies sometimes quoted parts of the classic poem on love, the thirteenth chapter of Paul's first letter to the Corinthians, concluding, as one put it, that "Paul's statement is comprehensive and goes further than anything to be heard so far in the debate on love."[3] It was a love that transcended all human divisions, or should: "Love the people you hate, for you should pity them—the cop who's full of animal fear. . . . Love the tortured souls who have all the material things, but nothing spiritual to make their lives bearable."[4]

This freely giving love was essentially a state of mind, but it was held to issue in ethical conviction, and thus love could become action: "It can change and create. It can move and it can shake moral, political, ethical, economic, and spiritual consciousness."[5] Applied love resulted in the practice of the Golden Rule and in concern for all beings. "We can do it, but it has to be 'WE'!!!!!! . . . all these lonely people need only someone to give a shit about them."[6] And this love was not merely a matter of creating some passing bit of goodness for a moment; if truly practiced, it would reform the world. It would counter the existing way of hate, epitomized by the politics of capitalists and communists alike, the politics of exploitation and war that had led the world to the brink of catastrophe.[7] Indeed, hippies argued, love was the *only* answer to the overwhelming problems afflicting the world. Applied love was the only way to human community, to a real solution to the world's seemingly intractable ills.

For most hippies, love meant nonviolence. Violence, they argued, was the product of a corrupt society and was one of that society's dead ends. "Violence is a means to itself only, ain't nothing good gonna come of it never. Never has, never will," went a typical hip pronouncement.[8] Thus the love ethic could be a bridge between the cultural hippies and the New Left politicos—the main agenda item of the New Left was, after all, ending the war in Vietnam, and what higher expression of love could there be than peace?

Love at its best was organized. The Diggers who surfaced in San Francisco and elsewhere and other similar groups were the prime model of organized love.[9] In an early statement, the Diggers announced that they were trying "to help motivate the youth who move about without direction, to discover the rich creative potential inherent in them and to establish positive goal-directed activities for themselves." To that end, they supplied "food and housing for those in need, not to create dependency, but as a starting point towards self-realization and independence," on the theory that the solution of individual problems pointed the way to the building of "the creative society we all desire."[10] Thus they gave away food to the public, ran free stores, and provided free places to sleep; they even undertook the huge task of feeding the thousands of people at the Be-Ins: "In the spirit of the Five Thousand, the Diggers began to feed the multitude," one hip reporter wrote concerning the first big Be-In.[11] Other groups did work along the same lines, among them the Provos of Berkeley[12] and the Church of Holy Water.[13]

But the hippies hardly achieved perfect love. They were human, after all, and therefore flawed; the more perceptive among them tempered idealism with realism. One wrote, "Perhaps we're no different from our parents after all. We're just stoned when we inflict pain upon our brothers."[14] Another speculated, "I think we have fallen prey to the sickness which we fight. We have begun to hate those who do not love and by so doing we have become those we fight against. . . . I say we need a true revolution. A revolution of non-violence and love."[15]

Many who seized the rhetoric of peace and love quickly perverted it. Protesting that perversion was the point of the funeral that marked the "Death of Hip" in San Francisco in the fall of 1967: the wave of love, or love-talk, was being usurped by many who did not know its spirit.[16] Sometimes the degradation of love was commercial, as when in the Haight-Ashbury an old greasy spoon became the "Love Cafe," serving "love burgers" and "love dogs," or when advertisers put together a "Love Guide," a map of Haight-Ashbury businesses. In another case, the "Love Conspiracy Commune" put on a "Love Circus" at $3.50 per head; it was picketed by Diggers and others who claimed that it was an "exploitation of love"—"if it's really love it would be free."[17] "There's nothing like a little love, and most Haight-Ashbury merchants are shucking it out by the truckload," wrote one counterculturist before the Summer of Love had even begun.[18]

Given the problems with the noble idea of love, perhaps it is not too surprising that some counterculturists found the entire idea hopeless. A few, at least, came to believe that love simply was not realistic in a world of militarism and hatred: "Tuning in to the flowers and to love and turning on to acid is very nice, but it's schizophrenia just like the suburban kind."[19]

The majority, however, were profoundly dedicated to peace and love. Love, after all, was all you needed.

✳ ✳ ✳ Political Ethics

Many of the most heartfelt hippies were decidedly cultural, not political, in their outlook, and they often chastized the New Left for its rather puritanical devotion to social change through political action. But the hippie lifestyle had political implications; persons living on the boundary of what was socially acceptable could not always avoid political reality, no matter what they thought of it.

Certainly the hippies had no one approach to politics. Two schools of thought dominated the fragmented field. One of those schools was that of disinvolvement, of dropping out of society, of refusing to participate in anything that smacked of politics, of avoiding dealing with the prevailing powers if at all possible;[20] the other was that of cultural revolution, of fighting in the social and political arena for reform of laws and mores that obstructed countercultural activities and occasionally for other humanitarian political ends, such as curbing private property rights. Relatively few hippies seemed to cling consistently to either of the two camps. Even such a prominent figure as Raymond Mungo, who, after his disavowal of activism, was virulently antipolitical, found it necessary to engage in a politics of confrontation when he refused military induction. Despite his skepticism that radical activity in any case would ever make any difference, he noted that "I've always been absolutely sure that every man who refuses induction is one less man in the Army, one more on the positive side of the chalk line."[21]

On the whole, disengagement was at least theoretically the more attractive pole for the counterculture. Two main arguments were advanced for that position. First, there was the cynical conviction that however right a political opinion might be, there was no use in trying to effect change, because it simply wouldn't work. As Mungo, the archetypal theoretician of cynicism, put it, "I am sufficiently tuned-in to the century to realize that we men never really get *anywhere*. It's always more of the same, so to speak—birth, life, death. . . . We do tend to end up where we started."[22] Some counterculturists had spent many years battling for civil rights, working to end the war in Southeast Asia, trying to reorder national economic priorities, attempting to reform the schools, and so forth, and they did not see any significant results for their considerable effort. Such short-term gains as there had been tended, they believed, to have been offset by a lack of long-term improvement.[23] In such circumstances, it was not difficult to sink into cynicism. Hippies with political experience had the feeling that they knew that of which they spoke and that they therefore had a finer insight on politics than did revolutionaries who had not yet seen the total uselessness of demonstrations and other political activities.[24] Even such a simple act as voting was often condemned as useless, or worse. "Voting is an illusory act. . . . Not once has a 'leader' been truthful to his 'people.' . . . Don't vote."[25]

Beyond cynicism, some argued that politics was simply not of concern to free people; cultural revolution did not involve political activity so much as it did simply being liberated. One "characteristic of the new revolutionist," a hippie wrote, "is that he is not content to wait for the revolution, is in his life style anticipating the revolution, is in a sense living the revolution."[26] Another concurred, "The age of politics is finished. . . . The only way you get freedom is by deciding that you're free. If you fight authority, you acknowledge it, you give it power. If authority is ignored, it doesn't exist any more."[27] To those who complained that change requires a political program, the counterculture replied, in the words of Ralph Gleason and Raymond Mungo,

> No, the hippies and the Beatles and the Pop musicians present no Program for Improvement of the Society. What they do is to present a program for improvement of the young people of the world. You can't change the society until you reach a state of grace. . . .[28]
>
> I no longer have any kind of program to save the world, let alone nineteenth-century Marxism, except perhaps to pay attention to trees. . . . I'll just go my solitary way and strive to enjoy what may well be the last days of this beautiful but deteriorating planet.[29]

Politics held no salvation for anyone; hope came only in life, in the lives of individuals and in that of freedom itself. "Power to no one. Life to everyone."[30]

Some writers saw dope as pointing the way to political disinvolvement. Dope was held to communicate to the user that "you don't overcome a negative force by opposing it directly on the level of force itself."[31] Beyond that, psychedelics frequently led the user to a new way of life lacking the leadership-oriented organization that is essential to conventional politics.

* * * Nature and the Environment

The counterculture harbored many early and articulate critics of the increasingly obvious and severe degradation of the environment that was taking place by the mid-1960s. Most popular hippie writings on the environment tended to be antitechnological and philosophically based on Eastern metaphysics and pieces of the Native-American tradition. The basic proposition was simple: human beings were an integral part of nature, not its masters, and one was thus obligated to adapt oneself to the flow of things instead of interfering with it and trying to conquer it, which was perceived to be the traditional Western way of dealing with nature. A fairly typical sentiment came from George Harrison: "The more you meditate and the more you harmonize with life in general then the more nature supports you."[32]

A 1967 list of "Ten commandments for getting to the city of God" published in the San Francisco *Oracle* included "Revere nature."[33] That could mean many things, including environmental activism, outdoor living, and opposition to experimentation on animals, among others.[34] Similarly Charles Reich, presenting a bill of seven particulars summarizing the nature of the American crisis to which he saw the hippies as responding, included in his list "Uncontrolled technology and the destruction of the environment."[35] But the bottom line for the counterculture was learning the ancient truth that the human race is finally only one tiny part of a huge nature, and that the race's survival depends on learning to live harmoniously with nature, not on conquering it or beating it back.

In the early days of the counterculture, in the middle 1960s, the perception that the earth itself was gravely endangered was still a bit of a novelty, not widely held as it is today. It was here, perhaps better than in any other place, that the ethics of the counterculture was visionary. Many derided hippies in the 1960s for their rather naive love of nature and sense of portending doom. A quarter of a century later they don't look quite so silly.

✳ ✳ ✳ Dropping Out

Closely related to the countercultural view of politics was the admonition (popularized as a slogan by Timothy Leary) to drop out, to quit Establishment society and drop into the New Age. It was a concept sufficiently important to the counterculture that Lewis Yablonsky included it as one of the ten points of his "Psychedelic Creed."[36]

Dropping out was to some extent political ("We are absolved from all Allegiance to the United States Government and all governments controlled by the menopausal," Leary wrote[37]), but it was broader than just that. It was the disowning of a life oriented toward work, status, and power; it was a search for poverty, simplicity, and new ideas.[38] Richard Alpert (later Baba Ram Dass) called it a reorganization of personal relations so as to make each moment meaningful.[39]

In some cases, dropping out was associated with the individualized search for truth and enlightenment that characterizes the lives of most of the great religious figures:

> A drop-out is a retrogression; the psychologists call it "positive disintegration." You drop out of the ego-addicting symbol attachment into the billion year old flow of electrical energy. You relinquish the I, Me and Mine of existence and expand into the selfless void of essence, not Mine, but thine. That is the message of all the great masters.
>
> Each man is his own Buddha, on his own trip. Find your own way of dropping out. . . . Remember, everything is progress.[40]

Thus the phenomenon of voluntary detachment from majority society had good historical precedent; for those Christians and Jews who denounced the ethic of dropping out, hippies noted that the observance of a Sabbath, "at least theoretically, is simply a weekly 'dropping out' from everyday activity for the purpose of reflection and spiritual renewal."[41]

Dropping out was more a concept than a program, for although a few hippies had independent means, most had to make a living. Only a few could be supported directly by hip culture—the dope dealers, a few of the musicians. So if only for economic reasons, most kept one foot firmly in Establishment society. Nevertheless, the sense of psychic separation from the mainstream was important. One knew that

one was free and, within the limits of the mundane needs of life, lived
that way.

✳ ✳ ✳ Money and Materialism

The Woodstock festival of 1969, as planned and temporary
as it was, was ever afterward idealized by hippies as a time and place
"free from the need of money,"[42] and thus a model for life in the New
Age. Counterculturists examined the money-based economic systems
of the world and found them wanting. Lawrence Lipton wrote in 1970,
"Moneytheism is a religion. It began as a religion and to this day it has
all the mythology and ritual that goes with religion. . . ."[43]

The hippies proclaimed what in a sense is obvious but few admit:
money itself is meaningless; it is, in the words of Alan Watts, so many
poker chips, without intrinsic value and (Watts argued) outdated in an
electronic age.[44] The problem, as Watts expressed the ethic that the
hippies embraced, is that most people confuse the artificial construct
that is money with wealth, which is "the sum of energy, technical intelligence and raw materials."[45]

The counterculture proved the depth of the entrenchment of that
confusion on several occasions. On the best publicized of them, Abbie
Hoffman, Jerry Rubin, and several others demonstrated their disdain
for money by throwing thirty or forty one-dollar bills (they claimed it
was a thousand) from the visitors' gallery onto the floor of the New
York Stock Exchange with the declaration, "Money is over."[46] The Exchange was sufficiently horrified to install a pane of glass at the front
of the gallery to prevent any recurrence of the outrage. Other similar acts elsewhere met with similar responses; the American public was
clearly not ready to follow Rubin's suggestion to "use your money as
toilet paper."[47]

Yet the counterculture was not entirely—or even mainly—free from
the lure of the allegedly evil artificial substance. Stewart Brand provided a clever case in point when, at the June 1971 party to celebrate
the demise of the original *Whole Earth Catalog* series, he tried to give
the 1,500 assembled people $20,000 on the sole condition that they
come to some agreement as to its use. Some wanted to divide it on the
spot; others came up with a range of proposals, none of which met

with general acceptance. Finally, the surviving $14,905 (the balance had already disappeared into the crowd) was entrusted to the one individual present who "seemed to hate money the most." The last report, months later, was that the individuals involved had a tentative plan to establish a "synergy warehouse" to "create an alternative urban environment," but the specifics were still lacking and nothing concrete had been done.[48] Brand had made his point well, that the antimoney counterculture was still very uptight about it all.

The hippies lived in the real world, but their ideal remained a disavowal of the materialism of American society. At the very least, they proclaimed a disavowal of consumer culture, believing, as Raymond Mungo wrote, that "a man with good boots on his feet and 9 dollars in his pocket can get most anything he needs in this world."[49] Money symbolized many evils; the materialism and greed that characterized America needed to give way to a new order "free from property hang-ups, free from success fixations, free from positions, titles, names, hierarchies, responsibilities, schedules, rules, routines, regular habits."[50] As Kenneth Keniston said, the counterculture sought "new *values for living,* values that will fill the spiritual emptiness created by material affluence."[51]

Mungo: "We never ask each other 'what do you *do?*' in the sense of 'how do you make money?' Many of us make no money at all, others do but it is something less than incidental to our lives, which are really about a million forces having nothing to do with career, profession, or money."[52]

Again, however, all this is either blue-sky romanticism or evidence of social privilege. Some of the hippies who talked the most about abolition of money were children of privilege for whom the grinding reality of real want was nonexistent. The poor rarely found their young turning into hippies.

✳ ✳ ✳ Work and Play

In a nation built on the Protestant ethic, the counterculture proclaimed the heresy that play was better than work. Play has, in fact, been held to be a central concept of the counterculture: as one hip theoretician put it,

There is one quality which enlivens both the political and cultural denominations of Youth protest; which provides its most important innovations; which has the greatest relevance for the future; which is the funniest, freakiest and the most effective. This is the element of play.[53]

Johan Huizinga, in his classic study of play, found freedom to be its major characteristic.[54] For the counterculture, freedom was important, but so was fun. Play "adorns life, amplifies it and is to that extent a necessity both for the individual—as a life function—and for society . . . as a cultural function."[55]

The counterculture differentiated play from organized athletics, which it saw as a "ritualized, legitimised aggression narcotic; hard work, competitive, corrupt."[56] The perfect countercultural game/sport was Frisbie, with no score keeping, no competition, no rules, and no apparent potential as a profitable spectator sport. (Those who eventually tried to make it a competitive sport thus profaned its essence.)

Play was seen as the wave of the future in that it offered a real alternative to the organization and regimentation that afflicted society. Those who failed to incorporate an element of play into their lives were missing out. Ron Jarvis wrote,

> One of the healthiest aspects, if not the core, of the young's defiance is its acceptance or its welcoming of pleasure and sensuality. No longer is it necessary for a revolutionary to be dour and severe. This outlook is what indicates the eventual success of our revolution over those of other times. No more guilt, no hideous neuroses or psychoses. Life is to be lived, not endured.[57]

Allen Ginsberg agreed: "Life should be ecstasy. We need life styles of ecstasy and social forms appropriate to whatever ecstasy is available for whoever wants it."[58]

The work ethic was distinctly distasteful to the hippies, and it was bashed head-on, as by Abbie Hoffman:

> Take W-O-R-K. When we say that nobody is going to work in the new world, it really spooks them. Not ideology nor drugs. W-O-R-K. When you tell the straight world you are never going to work again they go into ulcers.
>
> I think this is because W-O-R-K is directly linked to the Judeo-

Christian guilt complex. The original sin. W-O-R-K supposedly atones for all sins. The Protestant ethic has worked hand-in-hand with capitalism to keep the wheels rolling and the poor fuckers down in the mines.[59]

All of that does not mean that counterculturists were determined to never lift a finger again; what it did mean was that they were determined to avoid the slavery of drudgery, to change the situation in which, as Philip Slater wrote, "Technology makes core policy . . . and the humans adjust as best they can."[60] Charles Reich wrote that the counterculture was not opposed to work itself, but only to meaningless work, and that hippies worked as hard as anyone else at something they enjoyed doing—building a commune, constructing a people's park, pursuing a hobby.[61] Work directly related to pleasure and human needs became "work transformed," work that was fun to do.[62] As Tuli Kupferberg wrote,

> Believe me when I say: if you enjoy it, it can still be good; it can still be "work" (only we'll call it "play"). Play is as good as work. Work has been defined as something you *dislike* doing. Fuck that. Do the Beatles *work*? Who cares. We like what they do.[63]

One fundamental reason why the counterculture could reject work was that work seemed to be moving toward obsolescence. The counterculture had a sense that modern technology was becoming so productive that work, all the time, was no longer required of every member of society in order to supply the necessities of life. "The core of the old culture is scarcity," wrote Philip Slater, but scarcity no longer existed.[64] Without saying that scarcity could never come again, the hippies argued that at least in their time and place net scarcity existed only when it was artificially induced. Many existing jobs, they believed, were holdovers from the age of scarcity and thus totally useless. Eliminate the guards, customs agents, locksmiths, tax agents, salespersons, accountants, insurance agents, advertising agents, ticket agents, bankers, and all others whose jobs stem from scarcity, and a great deal of pointless human effort would be eliminated. And there was no need to worry about incentives, the hippies naively maintained; only a minority of the present work force would need to labor if all the useless jobs were eliminated. There would, in short, be plenty for all with minimal effort.[65]

One of the chief countercultural complaints against automation and cybernation was that those forces had dehumanized society by making people slaves to machines. The postscarcity point of view rehumanized technology without dismantling it. Kenneth Westhues argued that "the significance of the counterculture today is that it urges a break with the theory of rationalization in favor of the exciting possibilities a world created by rational thought permits."[66] And so in the counterculture, "automation has replaced work, play assumes its rightfully central role."[67]

✳ ✳ ✳ Ripping Off the Establishment

Most ethical systems include a fairly straightforward prohibition of theft. In general, the counterethics included such a prohibition. But in a few instances a case was made for a Robin Hood approach to stealing: there could be a moral justification for stealing from the rich.

In general, stealing was justifiable in the counterculture only if it was at the expense of those who were perceived to have stolen—legally or not—to get their wealth in the first place. But one could drive a semitrailer truck through that loophole, as Jerry Rubin did: "All money represents theft. To steal from the rich is a sacred and religious act. To take what you need is an act of self-love, self-liberation."[68] Beyond that, some hippies justified stealing by arguing that capitalism produced economic irrationality. When surpluses existed in a world of hungry people, stealing from the surplus could not be evil.[69]

In some cases, hippies provided their peers with specific advice on methods of stealing from the corporate thieves. A series of articles in the *East Village Other* outlined several possibilities: getting free new-account gifts from banks by devious means; "losing" traveler's checks to double one's money; "losing" a credit card; giving false credit card numbers in telephoned business transactions; and flying with airline tickets that had been reported stolen.[70] In several instances, detailed instructions were provided for the fradulent use of telephone credit card numbers.[71] Most of this information and much more was detailed in Abbie Hoffman's guerilla manual, *Steal This Book*.[72]

One sophisticated form of the ripoff was record and tape bootlegging. Protesting the high prices and alleged monopolistic practices of the record companies, bootleggers sometimes operated in violation of copyright and contractual rights of artists and producers. In most cases, their products were of relatively low quality and high price, but the largest, Rubber Dubber Records (with 37 employees), claimed to operate "under a strict code of business ethics" that included the use of only the best vinyl, a guarantee of quality, a price held to $6 per double album, and the payment of a royalty (25 cents per record) to artists. Rubber Dubber contended that its business was legal, ethical, and necessary to the counterculture.[73]

✳ ✳ ✳ Hair, Obscenity, Dirt

It would seem frivolous, at best, to enunciate an ethic of hair, or profanity, or dirt, but the hippies did just that, largely in self-defense against those who saw hopeless degeneracy in the counterculture's approach to such matters.

Hair was one of the most visible symbols of the culture of opposition. It provided a name of a smash musical about the countercultural lifestyle and the name of at least one underground newspaper (in Minneapolis, ca. 1969). Why did hippies grow their hair long? Primarily as a symbol of separateness, or, as Richard Neville put it, as a countercultural declaration of independence.[74] "Long hair, beards, no bras and freaky clothes represent a break from Prison Amerika."[75] Indeed, for some time, hippies loved to call themselves "freaks."

The counterculture deemed it equally important to ask why American society was critical of long hair, pointing out that most recent mass murderers were short-haired and that major (especially organized) criminals were usually short-haired and beardless. One writer suggested that the naked ape might possibly feel superior to longhairs because he or she considered the latter throwbacks to the earlier stages of the evolution of the species.[76] At any rate, if people worried about the length of things, they would be better advised to concern themselves about the length of the "lying tongues of politicians."[77]

The underground papers generally missed one broader implication of long hair, that of the apparent countercultural tendency toward androgynous appearance.[78] Conscious or not, androgyny was important and helped buttress hip ideas about unity and wholeness. Men grew hair that made them look more feminine, while women wore clothing, especially pants, that had a distinctly masculine air. (It is worth noting here that the counterculture apparently had a lot to do with freeing women to dress in pants; until the time of the hippies, skirts were the rule for women in all but the most informal settings.)

According to Mircea Eliade, androgyny reflects a dissatisfaction with one's actual situation (cut off from power and divinity) and a wish to recover this lost unity.[79] Thus countercultural androgyny in regard to hair and dress may have reflected the "traditional conception that one cannot be anything *par excellence* unless one is at the same time the opposite."[80]

"Obscene" language was the coin of the countercultural realm; the four-letter words first widely used publicly and unabashedly in the hip era were held to have had two main uses: through their shock value they constituted "a symbolic protest against middle-class hypocrisy," and in their frequent explicit sexualness they raised sexual discourse "above the ground in the hope of bringing sex with them—to put sex on the healthful, wholesome, beautiful" plane where it belonged.[81] The Establishment's disdain for "obscenity" helped promote its use in the counterculture; but, in any event, it soon became so widely used that it simply reflected a rejection of "propriety." Hippies believed that society had a misplaced sense of shock:

> What is obscene?
>
> Is it obscene to fuck, or
> Is it obscene to kill?
>
> Is it more obscene to describe fucking,
> An act of love, or
> Is it more obscene to describe killing,
> An act of hate?
>
> Are pictures of a nude person just fucked
> More or less obscene
> Than pictures of a dead person just killed?
>
> * * *
>
> Why does the church
> Condemn fucking,

An act which creates life, but
Condone killing
An act which takes life?

Why does the church consider it more heinous
For an American soldier to
Fuck
      an eighteen year old unmarried American girl than to
Kill
      an eighteen year old unmarried Vietnamese girl . . . ?
Why do children learn, at too young an age, that
The biggest no-no in the English language is   Fuck
While at the same tender age, or younger, learn that
Hate   and   kill
Are two of the most acceptable words in the English
     language. . . ?

What is really obscene?

Answer that question, and you will
Discover not only your own true values, but also
Where the true values of our
Christian natures lie.[82]

Finally, hippies were often condemned for appearing to be dirty.
Most of them saw bodily dirt as a morally neutral matter, but they perceived substantial irony (or worse) in the fact that their critics were
usually among those who consented to pollution, slums, and trash on
the airwaves. "That a few Hippies appear dirty punctuates the fact that
in a crucial sense all adult non-Hippies are filthy."[83]

✳ ✳ ✳ Hedonism

A notable difference between the counterethics and conventional Judaeo-Christian ethics came at the point of deliberate pleasure. The counterculture maintained as a "basic idea" that "pleasure
is good, and not immoral."[84] That had the effect of creating a "hedonistic gap" which, according to Timothy Leary, was "the real problem
of the world today."[85] Leary was a notable theoretician of hedonism,

proposing to raise the "hedonic index" of persons through "hedonic engineering," which he defined as "designing one's life for pleasure through chemical turn-ons and turn-offs."[86] Hedonism was morally valid, said Leary: it meant "living for pleasure instead of living according to the punishment-reward system that an up-tight society wants to keep us all trapped in."[87]

> An anti-hedonic society is an uptight society, is a punishment society and it's a warlike society, and we just can't afford that any more if we're going to survive as a species.
>
> The only issue today, as in the past, is the hedonic gap. Every issue, whether it's a psychological conflict, personality conflict, or social-political conflict always comes down to a hedonic gap.
>
> Some people try to bring others down or make them feel worse; the innate struggle of every individual is that he wants to feel better.[88]

Leary saw hedonism largely in terms of dope; others saw it more broadly. Country Joe McDonald once said, "Probably the most revolutionary thing in the U.S. right now is hedonism. By that I don't mean wasting your life away, but doing something that you enjoy. That really puts them uptight."[89] The Sexual Freedom League based much of its rationale for existence on hedonism: "If the pleasure principle is more operative in our lives, the anxiety principle would become less operative. Overall we would be less hostile, more capable of sentiment, affection and love."[90] And if there needed to be a moral justification for hedonism, there were two: the belief that morals were relative, not absolute, and the "saving importance of experience."[91]

William Braden criticized the counterculture at the point of hedonism on strategic grounds: hedonism could enslave as easily as liberate, and a technetronic dictatorship could rely on bread and circuses to pacify the masses.[92] But to the counterculture that was essentially a political argument, a contention that one should deny oneself pleasure for some very hypothetical political possibilities. True hippies could not allow politics to override pleasure.

✳ ✳ ✳ Truth, Honesty, Simplicity

Paul Krassner once said, "I don't believe in the biblical concept, 'Ye shall know the truth and the truth shall make you free,' because people have such a fantastic capacity to rationalize the truth."[93] That sort of rationalization, which is closely tied to hypocrisy, was consistently one of the main things that the counterculture criticized in majority society. The counterculture saw itself as "struggling to RISE FROM A SOCIETY which has adjusted to levels of moral and intellectual depravity, as low as its level of physical comfort is high."[94] Ralph J. Gleason epitomized the argument:

> Two long-haired kids in a sleeping bag on the fairgrounds is fornication; two crewcut kids after the high school dance in a motel is "sexual experience" and their parents, swapped around in a luxury hotel, is "making love."
>
> It is all right to drink whiskey and run a car into a tree. It is morally wrong to smoke grass and listen to music.[95]

The sin was not so much in the act as in the attitude. The counterculture proposed the elimination of double standards; it proposed a forthright honesty in daily life that it saw sadly lacking in most of society.

✳ ✳ ✳ Rationality

The counterculture that rejected technology as a god also rejected the Western rationality that underlies technology. The counterculture proposed an approach to life not of irrationality but of arationality, a disregard of the question of reasonableness. Reason had not answered any of the important questions of life, all of which lay on another plane; furthermore, arationality was part of human nature. "Logical argument doesn't work. People's heads don't work logically. People are emotion freaks. People are crazy."[96] Symbolically, "Words are the absolute in horseshit."[97] The counterculture was eros while Establishment, technological culture was logos. The counterculture was the virgin, technological culture the computer. The counterculture was spirit, technological culture reason.[98] There were not merely minor differences in viewpoint; hippies saw them as symptoms of the vast gulf between the two outlooks on life and culture.

Theodore Roszak wrote at length in forceful refutation of the rational, of objective consciousness, contending that Western culture's insistent dependence on "objectivity" vastly diminished its quality of life and, in fact, hindered a rapport with the world rather than helping it.[99] As Roszak notes, the counterculture was not entirely original in this critique, but helped popularize it:

> Theosophists and fundamentalists, spiritualists and flat-earthers, occultists and satanists . . . it is nothing new that there should exist anti-rationalist elements in our midst. What *is* new is that a radical rejection of science and technological values should appear so close to the center of our society, rather than on the negligible margins.[100]

In the counterculture there was little use for objective knowledge (beyond the development of a few simple tools for living, such as cooking, sewing, and primitive building); there was believed to be no overall nature of things in the rational sense. As Paul Goodman put it, everything could be reduced to interpersonal relations and power.[101] At that point, the fruits of reason turn sour.

CHAPTER 7

Legacy

Like, two years ago you could walk down the street and see a guy who looked real weird . . . and you knew. Now, I look out here and, well, everyone looks weird. You just can't tell anymore.

—Janis Joplin, *Great Speckled Bird*, 21 July 1969

A generation later, America is a different place than it was in the days of hip. Capitalism and what's-in-it-for-me? values are stronger than ever. There is no flowering counterculture, no vital New Left, no innovative rock and roll, no generational consciousness—and not much of a sense of enchantment or wonder in any part of society. Peace and love and flower power are no longer standard argot. Dope has given way to drugs; dynamic new music has given way to formula sound; the sexual revolution was slowed by herpes and then stopped in its tracks by AIDS. More broadly, the imagination that so character-ized the sixties—the optimistic and naive anticipation that the world was moving into an age of Aquarian harmony and understanding—seems utterly gone in a time when leading public figures want to clamp down on artistic expression, when the political world seems to have no leaders with vision or imagination, when cynical materialistic self-indulgence rules the land, when grim environmental realities render the future of the race unpredictable. In many ways hip culture has bloomed and died like a century plant, spectacularly but only once in a lifetime. On the other hand, the new ethics of the hippies has left last-ing traces in the culture, even if the vision of revolutionary upheaval has clearly not come to pass.

✳ ✳ ✳ The Counterethics: Just How New Was It?

The hippies fervently believed that what they were about was something entirely new. The past was rejected, forgotten; with the dawning of the age of Aquarius an entirely new consciousness was entering the human race, and the hippies were the vanguard of a revolutionary future which would inevitably sweep the world.

The claim that everything hip was new was hardly on the mark, however. Actually, the counterethics had three strata: a reaffirmation of some very traditional ideas and values; a championing of ideas that had been around for some time but were unfamiliar to or unaccepted by the majority; and, yes, some ideas that seem to have been truly original, or at least quite unusual in an American setting.

The Reaffirmation of Traditional Ethical Precepts. Much of the counterethics simply reaffirmed time-tested American values and tendencies, albeit sometimes in new clothing. The valuing of community in a country of individualists is an example of that. Americans have always been great champions of individualism; it was in America that the Bill of Rights was adopted, spelling out the rights of the individual to a degree unthinkable to most of the world of two centuries ago. Yet those individualistic Americans have always been participants, volunteers, community dwellers. As Henry Steele Commager once wrote, "For all his individualism, the American was much given to cooperative undertakings and to joining." [1] The hippies did their own thing, but a key part of the hip vision was generational community.

The hippies were iconoclasts, but iconoclasm is another classic American virtue. Americans early on slaughtered sacred cows—rejecting, for example, traditional government (monarchy), the traditional relationship of church and state, and a formal social class structure. In the nineteenth century, a gaggle of traditional institutions—slavery, the subordination of women, the use of alcohol as a beverage, and others—found themselves under attack by a new generation of reformers. The iconoclasm of the hippies was distinctive only in that new icons came under attack. Slavery and monarchy had already been abolished; the new gods assaulted by the counterculture were rationality, technocracy, and materialism.

Rural romanticism and the desire to protect the earth were also simply new expressions of old instincts. The disavowal of big cities as corrupt and unlivable has been a popular cultural theme for well over a century. Although massive environmental pollution was a new part of the equation in the hip era, the desire to flee to the country was not. The establishment of thousands of communes in rural areas was a replay of the agrarian ideal—not to mention a communal vision—which was well established in the nineteenth century.[2]

Finally, even in its methodological preference for pursuing social change by appealing to Americans' gut feelings, the counterculture was quite traditional. The hippies never worked very hard at trying to change institutions; their appeal was always to the heart. How do we change society? Well, if enough individuals are transformed, then society will inevitably follow. The hippies were convinced that American society was so degenerate that no scheme of structural changes could possibly succeed; the only hope for a better tomorrow was to drop out, to disaffiliate from society and encourage others to do the same. If enough drop out, then and only then will a new consciousness dominate society. That appeal—heartfelt and to the heart—is one Americans have made from the beginning.

The Espousal of Existing Minority Positions. In rejecting the ideas and values of majority society, the hippies in many cases adopted points of view that had already been articulated by a social minority. In some cases, a particular school of thought was thus given wide exposure for the first time; and, for that reason, the hippies seemed to be proclaiming something really new when they weren't.

Sexual freedom is a case in point. There have long been individuals and groups who deviated from the established patterns of heterosexuality, monogamy, marriage, and wearing clothes, but they have tended to be few and their voices weak. Albert Ellis, for example, has been writing and lecturing in favor of sexual freedom for decades; but prior to the coming of the counterculture, ideas like his were hardly the coin of the realm. Similarly there have long been organizations of nudists who have taken off their clothes in the interest of better health and communion with nature, but only with the hippies, for whom nudity meant fun and freedom, did disrobing attract widespread attention.

The hippie precept of dropping out of the larger society to seek a purer life was not a new one, nor was it novel to create communes in the country for those who wanted to live among like-minded drop-outs. Certainly some of the early European settlers in America were malcontents who saw themselves as having to withdraw from society and head for the wilderness to find satisfaction. Communes were there from the seventeenth century onward, reaching a major peak in the early nineteenth century. The grand communes of that era were often founded in locations far from major cities and represented dissatisfaction with the existing social arrangements. The hippies saw themselves as creating new family structures in their communes, but that had been done fairly extensively in the first half of the nineteenth century. The Shakers, for example, saw themselves as living in families of a new type; "family" was the name of the largest subunit in each of the Shaker villages. The Oneida Community of John Humphrey Noyes saw itself as a single family with hundreds of members; in its system of complex marriage each woman and each man in the community were regarded as spouses.

Finally, the rejection of materialism, consumerism, and the mindless exploitation of the planet were all old themes, which prior to the hippies had never had widespread followings. There have always been hermits and members of religious orders who have rejected the dominant culture's material and commercial values, but in possession- and money-mad America they have been few indeed. Similarly there have been those who have argued for the preservation of nature for at least a century and a half, but until recently the majority of Americans have been more interested in conquering than in preserving nature. The hippies were part of a cultural vanguard when they argued that the earth needed to be protected, not exploited.

New Ethical Ideas. Not many ideas are entirely new, but some cherished ethical positions of the hippies were at least distinctive and newly refined. Probably the most important counterethical position that could be regarded as essentially new was the positive embracing of what the majority society lumps into the pejorative category of "drugs." There have been "drug cults" in other times and places ranging from ancient India to contemporary Native-American Society, but the counterculture was taking a position new to just about every Euro-American when it argued that heretofore forbidden psychoactive substances could and should be used for pleasure and spiritual insight. (Yes, many have championed the legitimacy of the use of alcohol, America's perennial favorite drug; but it has hardly been argued that alcohol *should* be universally used for exhilaration and introspection.) The hippies believed that dope, universally used, would effect a change of consciousness that would be enormously beneficial to the world. That argument represented a novel point of view.

The promotion of an ethic of fun and play was relatively new in America as well. What is usually termed the Protestant work ethic has dominated the land for centuries; the only people who really aren't expected to work are the rich (and even they would be better off working) and the unfit. In the face of that cultural tradition, the hippies argued that work was not necessary, modern technological culture being sufficiently productive that it could carry a fair number of nonproducers without undue burden on the rest. Pleasure was no longer to be regarded as demonic; now it was an essential ingredient of the free life. Hedonism, in disrepute in the West since perhaps the time of the Epicureans, was once again an ethical imperative.

Finally, the rejection of rationality and of the whole concept of objective consciousness was an important component of the counterethics and a distinctive one. There have in the past been antirationalists in America, but usually they have opposed only one part of science and/ or rationality, as in the case of flat-earthers; and they have also been socially marginal. Although the spirit of rationality is so thoroughly embedded in American culture that it can hardly be escaped entirely, the counterculture worked steadily against it. Devotion to reason, the counterculture argued, has dehumanized life by downplaying emotion; it has made slaves of persons and has essentially contradicted human nature, which is not entirely rational.

✳ ✳ ✳ The Impact of the Counterculture on Society, Then and Now

The hippies were cultural shock troops. Unlike some other dissenters before them, they were often recognizable on sight, with their long hair, flowers and beads, colorful clothing, painted vehicles, and the like. Their ideas were widely if imperfectly known; suddenly with widespread public awareness of a counterculture came a huge national debate over recreational drugs, liberated sexuality, rock music, private property, and other topics raised for public debate by the hippies.

Did they have any effect, either transitory or long lasting, on members of society who never considered themselves hippies? Certainly they seem to have had an impact in their own time. It was the hippies who popularized recreational drugs among a wide swath of the population. Dope had been around before, particularly in certain circles of artists and musicians and in various racial subcultures. But never before had it spread so widely through the culture. By 1972 more than 40 percent of the American college-student population had tried marijuana; and, in all, an estimated twenty-four million Americans had used the illegal weed.[3] Such large populations never tried LSD or other forms of dope; but, nevertheless, the spread of the smorgasbord of drugs was unprecedented. One survey conducted in 1974 and 1975 found that 22 percent of a national sample of men aged twenty to thirty had used psychedelic chemicals, and 7 percent were using them regularly at the time of the survey.[4] More recently, a 1989 survey concluded that over seventy million Americans, close to 30 percent of the population, had used one or more illicit drugs at some time in their lives, and that nearly thirty-seven million had done so in the last year.[5]

Similarly widespread was a new attitude toward sex. Premarital sex became much more widely and openly practiced than ever before, and tolerance of sexual expressions other than genital-to-genital marital heterosex increased to some extent. Homosexuals began asserting their rights publicly for the first time. Surveys showed major changes in American attitudes toward sex. As late as 1969, the Gallup Poll found that only 21 percent of American adults approved of premarital intercourse, while 68 percent condemned it;[6] but by the time the new thinking had had a chance to percolate through the culture, that had changed dramatically. A 1977 survey conducted by Yankelovich, Skelly, and White found that only 34 percent of those under twenty-five believed that it was wrong for teenagers to engage in sexual intercourse; of the whole population, 52 percent believed that it was not morally wrong for an unmarried man and woman to live together, and 56 percent favored civil rights for homosexuals. Asked how their views on sexual morality had changed, 41 percent said that their views had become more liberal, while only 15 percent had become more conservative.[7]

One can argue that sexual liberation would have happened without the hippies; it happened that the hip era came on the heels of such revolutionary cultural developments as the widespread dissemination of oral contraceptives in the early 1960s, the achievement of effective treatment of venereal diseases through antibiotics, and the development of private locations for sexual activity outside the parental home (notably in the universalization of the automobile). Even stipulating the independent emergence of new options, however, the counterculture played an important role in popularizing the new freedom and especially in enunciating the ethics that made it all acceptable.

There were lesser, often transitory impacts as well. For a time in the 1970s, hippie ideas about appearance had some influence on the larger society. Longer hair and more colorful clothing for men were in vogue for a few years. Widespread acceptance of casual clothing, especially blue jeans, now seems well entrenched. In many circles, it is no longer odd to hear once-forbidden four-letter words. But such things were and are peripheral to the central message of the counterculture except insofar as they represent some general acceptance of the hippie value of self-expressiveness.

The matter of the long-term impact of the hippies is not an easy one to judge. The counterculturists themselves believed that they were on the cutting edge of a true cultural revolution, that the world would be changed forever by the new consciousness they were bringing. As Allen Ginsberg responded, when asked in 1969 whether hippies might revert to the middle class as they grew older,

> No; impossible. . . . The way's been barred by beatings and arrests. What bridges they haven't burned behind them have been burned for them with pot busts. What's happened to young people is a sudden breakthrough catalyzed in part by psychedelic drugs. Another factor was the deconditioning caused by alienation from social authority as it proved itself completely incomprehensible and mad and burned its own bridges from Hiroshima to Vietnam.[8]

One scenario popular among the hippies was that their ultimate cultural triumph was inevitable, that the ideas and ethics of the counterculture would soon predominate in society at large. That vision is the essential point of Charles Reich's *The Greening of America*. Naturally many writers in the hip press expressed the conviction that hip ideas would dominate the world. John Gabree, for example, writing in 1971, saw the counterculture leading the society to true peace (a society without war or institutionalized violence), equality, and love (a society that would respect the humanity of everyone, and would celebrate truthfulness and compassion), even if getting there from here still entailed "a hell of a lot of work."[9] And some saw it as simply coming, hard work or no; as Tom Wolfe wrote, the world seemed to be living with a "millennium at hand, and it *is*, because there's no earthly stopping this thing. It's like a boulder rolling down a hill—you can watch it and talk about it and scream and say Shit! but you can't stop it. It's just a question of where it's going to go."[10]

Others were less optimistic about the ultimate conversion of the world to hip thinking but believed nevertheless that hip would become permanently established as a way of life for an enlightened minority. Raymond Mungo spoke for that position:

> If we live long enough to create it, the New Age will be *peace on earth*. The judicious strife we now suffer on earth must be related to and seen in the light of that Kool Space which will make it an ancient chapter in our development. At the risk of adopting missionary zeal, we ought to go back to the cities and bring out the young and alienated, to the land and peace, "save" them in a sense from the death of the body and soul amid the glitter of better ketchup bottles and new Buicks.

> The peace we find in Kool Space will give us the internal strength to move in the Old Age, in the cities, for example, without succumbing to it; the peace in the New mentality is a peace without adequate words ("notoriously non-linear these hippies," says the latest *New York Review*) and we should seek to turn on and carry away the prospective new people rather than merely convince them.

> Free from material need, unconcerned for what used to be called "poverty," we will escape the poisons of the city, which itself inhibits our revolution and warps our art. The cities of America are unnecessary evils in an age of electronic communication and transportation; they will become hollow museums to our past,

burned down by the poor during the last gasp of the Old Age and now echoing with the sharp footsteps of the occasional, amused visitor. There is Kool Space enough for all of us—*look up today, rather than down*.[11]

Such was the vision, but not exactly the reality. The wave of sixties-nostalgia literature which mushroomed in the late 1980s generally regarded it as all over. There have been endless newspaper feature stories on former hippies who now carry briefcases, on a new generation of "serious" college students, on the national mania for trivial but expensive material possessions. The era of the hippies and the New Left was a colorful and chaotic one, but in the long run it hasn't made much of an impact on the larger society: such is the conventional wisdom.

Have the changes in American attitudes and activities that apparently followed the heyday of the counterculture vanished? It seems clear enough, as we saw a few pages ago, that by the middle 1970s, in the wake of the counterculture, Americans had become more permissive about sexual activity and drug use; certainly the hippies had made some impact on style, what with widespread popularity of longer hair on men, colorful and casual clothing, the casual use of once-forbidden words, the evolution of icons and artifacts (peace signs, coke spoons) into jewelry, and a hundred other things. But has the impact vanished? Is America today no different than it would have been had the legendary generational revolt never occurred? With materialism, capitalism, and sheer greed as rampant in America as they have ever been, is there no legacy at all?

Well, no. Things are not entirely as they were before. There is at least some ongoing impact in the three most renowned centers of the hip revolution: sex, dope, and rock and roll. Further, one can make the case that the growing national concern for the environment follows up on an alarm which the hippies were among the first to sound. And the hip rebellion has left its imprint on other parts of American life, such as the spread of the cult of the body and the movement toward socially responsible investing.

Americans continue to be more tolerant of liberal sexual mores than they were before the hippies arrived on the scene. According to a 1987 Gallup report, the percentage of Americans saying that premarital sex is wrong dropped from 68 in 1969 to 39 in 1985 before climbing back to 46 in 1987. For the eighteen to twenty-nine year-olds, 49 percent had called premarital sex wrong in 1969, versus 18 percent in 1985 and 27 percent in 1987. A similar shift had occurred in the oldest age group in the sample, persons over fifty: 80 percent in 1969 said that premarital sex was wrong, 56 percent in 1985, and 65 percent in 1987. Those numbers would suggest that the loosening of sexual ideology in the late 1960s has finally run its course, that old sexual standards are returning. But the pollsters specifically doubted that conclusion, noting in their report that disease may be "a key factor" in the reversal that seems to have set in recently.[12]

A more honest reversal may have come about on the dope front—especially if, as seems plausible, attitudes toward the use of marijuana are a fair indicator. Another Gallup report, this one in 1985, concluded that the "groundswell of public opinion in the mid-1970's toward more liberal marijuana laws appears to have run its course." In 1977, 66 percent of Americans sampled (46 percent of those between eighteen and twenty-nine) opposed legalization of pot; in 1985, 73 percent of the population (66 percent of the younger set) had that opinion. Only among the college educated was there any shift toward liberalization, with 71 percent in 1977 opposing legalization and 68 percent in 1985 opposing it. Statistically, that amounts to little change. By 1985, 50 percent of the population believed that the possession of small amounts of marijuana should be criminal, with 46 percent disagreeing, whereas in earlier samplings "in 1980 and 1977, small majorities backed *removal* of criminal penalties for possession."[13] It would be hard to argue from any body of data that America had not moved toward a harder line against drugs two decades after the heyday of hip. Indeed, a 1987 Roper poll found that when Americans were asked to name two or three things they were most concerned about, drug abuse led the list, with 43 percent naming it. Lower on the list of concerns were such things as crime (36 percent) and foreign relations (27 percent). A Gallup poll taken about the same time found a similar ranking of priorities, but with lower numbers: drug abuse was ranked as one of the "most important problems" for the nation by 11 percent, second to unemployment (13 percent), and ahead of such things as the threat of war (7 percent), and poverty and hunger (5 percent). Astoundingly,

Americans responding to both polls apparently regarded drugs as a much greater threat than nuclear weapons![14]

In the case of rock music, it would be hard to argue that the music of the hip era is not still felt today. Indeed, the identical music retains a fair popularity, not only among the aging hippies but among a younger generation: no one who turns on a radio can fail to hear Beatles music frequently. When the remaining countercultural bands tour, their concerts are thronged—thousands at this writing continue to turn out for Grateful Dead concerts, and there is probably no hotter ticket in the business than the Rolling Stones. In 1989, the Stones, Bob Dylan, the Who, Paul McCartney, Ringo Starr, and the Dead were all touring and still eclipsing everything else musical that had come along in the two decades since their rise to popularity. Beyond that, however, the rock that the hippies saw as revolutionary has remained the fountainhead of a musical genre with an enormous following today. Some of it has become unimaginative and formulaic; some of it, such as punk and thrash, has gone in directions of its own. Its source in the sixties rock revolution is, however, undeniable.

Other hip themes have continued to resonate in the larger culture. Prominent among them is the cult of the body, which at this writing permeates much of America. Hordes of Americans jog and swim, and pour into thousands of health centers, and buy millions of workout videotapes. Eating healthy food has gone from being the fanaticism of a few cranks to a concern central to the lives of millions; and the whole American food industry is struggling to accommodate the surge in demand for wholesome, chemical-free foodstuffs. Many a suburban family now has food concerns that were once the province of the far-out hippies. Thus there is some plausibility to Craig Dremann's argument that food will be the longest lasting of all hip innovations:

> I can't think of anyone who began eating whole-wheat bread and then went back to white bread. While most of the folks who once thought of themselves as hippies have dropped their overt identification with hippie culture, they still partake of it by the food they eat. They eat hippie food—yogurt, carob, and so on— almost all of which was introduced into the "white-bread" culture by the original aboriginal hippie culture. . . . I imagine that five

hundred years from now about the only lasting cultural contribution that will be attributed to hippies will be the new plant foods and plant uses they introduced.[15]

Growing along with concern for health and nutrition has been the New Age movement, a vague and virtually indefinable collection of spiritual and somatic beliefs and practices with obvious roots in hippie culture. Many New Age schools focus on spiritual growth; many of them see spiritual, mental, and bodily growth as necessarily integrated. Practices ranging from massage, to the use of crystals, to alternative medical treatment, to astrology, to communication with persons on other planes have wide followings. While some New Age precepts are actually very old, their recent popularity seems to have received an important boost from the hippies. The New Age movement is not a very pure preservation of hippiedom; as Andrew Kimbrell has observed, the New Age movement has focused on individual, not social, transformation; and a visionary quest for personal alternatives without compassion for the oppressed is only a fragment, even a parody, of the hip agenda.[16] Nevertheless, the New Age movement is probably the most substantial remnant of hip culture we have.

Since hippiedom flowered a generation ago, the denizens of the counterculture are inevitably reaching ages when they are needing to make important financial decisions, especially in planning for retirement. It should not be surprising, therefore, that there is currently a growing movement toward socially responsible investing. The hippies generally proclaimed rather Buddhist ideas about work and money: one should have a right livelihood, and one should use one's resources for the promotion of the good. In the late 1960s and early 1970s, ethical questions regarding investments usually focused on college campuses: the demand was that college endowments divest themselves of holdings in businesses selling armaments or operating in South Africa, to cite only two controversial situations. As former hippies and their sympathizers have acquired some assets of their own, they have often clung to the ideal of investing them in a progressive fashion. Whole mutual funds and money-market funds have been created as vehicles for socially oriented investments, and even some major traditional financial firms have begun to cater to this growing market.

A related development is the growth of deliberately socially conscious business enterprises that try fairly deliberately to apply the hip vision to the workplace. Perhaps the best-known example of that at this writing is Ben and Jerry's ice cream company in Vermont. As many articles in the popular press have noted with some wonderment,[17] Ben and Jerry's employees can choose which jobs they want to do, get benefits including profit sharing, college tuition, and free ice cream—and work for a company that is serious about its environmental responsibilities and donates 7.5 percent of its pretax profits to progressive social causes. The hip vision of meaningful, socially responsible work may yet come to pass!

To some extent, the counterculture could be said to have helped stimulate the rekindled feminist movement of the last third of the twentieth century. The counterculture was largely male defined, but it tried to be inclusive, and caring about people was one of its basic themes. In their broad-spectrum challenge to the prevailing American way of doing things, the hippies did not fail to criticize traditional family life, which inevitably included sharply restrictive ideas about the roles women could play in society. Much of the new feminism of the 1970s was spearheaded by women who had logged at least some time among the hippies, and they reflected the hip critique of mainstream society in their assault on the discrimination women had historically faced.

Perhaps the most enduring legacy of the counterculture is the role that it played in awakening public concern about the environmental crisis of the late twentieth century. The hippies were nature-lovers, and many of them admired the American Indians whom they saw as, among other things, fine stewards of the natural world. From the beginning, one strain—small at first, but vocal—of the hippie critique of American culture was that it was fouling its nest, that for the sake of profit and convenience the survival of the world itself was severely at risk. As Roderick Nash has written in *The Rights of Nature*,

One of the most characteristic ideas of the 1960s concerned the need for fundamental changes in American life and thought. At its deepest level, the so-called counterculture advocated a new morality and the wholesale dismantling of many established institutions. The decade began with an emphasis on human rights, but by its end, as perception of an environmental crisis increased, the stakes began to widen to include nature.[18]

The whole notion of the nation's—and the world's—having grave environmental problems was still a new one in the late sixties, and one widely disbelieved; Rachel Carson's *Silent Spring*, the book that first focused widespread attention on the looming environmental catastrophe had only been published in 1962.[19] Hippies were deeply involved in the first Earth Day, 22 April 1970. As new and more radical environmental organizations (Greenpeace, Friends of the Earth, Earth First!) began to emerge during and after the hip era, they were often populated by individuals whose consciousness had been raised in the counterculture; and they often took their organizational and strategic cues from the hippies and the New Left. It is a safe guess that today veterans of the counterculture are disproportionately represented in the organizations fighting to turn back the tide of environmental degradation. While one cannot say that the hippies are solely responsible for widespread awareness of the environmental threat, surely their role in sounding alarums was an important one.

In sum, some footprints remain, while others seem to be fading. Long-range projections are difficult; who can say that if the AIDS epidemic is suddenly halted, sexual activity may not become freer than ever, or that some new route to pleasure will not capture the imagination of a subculture the way LSD and marijuana once did?

✷ ✷ ✷ Is the Legacy a Nightmare?

In a time of devastating sexually transmitted diseases and a widespread belief that drugs are tearing the social fabric apart, was the counterethics simply a curse? Do AIDS, and crack, and armies of homeless persons constitute the essential legacy of the counterculture?

No simple answer works very well here. The hippies were key agents in the blossoming of a drug culture, but somehow only part of the hip message managed to penetrate the larger society. The hippies advocated the use of dope, but the drugs that seem to be so destructive in America today aren't what the counterculturists called "dope." Crack is cocaine, not LSD or marijuana. To the hip ethical theorists, cocaine was one of those things (heroin was another) that entered the scene once acceptance of psychoactive substances had spread widely and helped destroy the visionary world of psychedelia. So hip permissiveness opened the door to the destruction of hip, as well as to problems elsewhere.

But the shift from dope to drugs does not tell the whole story either. Once dope had been defined, it still had to be used properly: set and setting were crucial components of the experience. Dope trips were ideally taken in positive, supportive company by persons who believed that something akin to religious revelation, or at least something very fun, could come from the experience. By comparison, neither set nor setting is right for the typical user of heroin or crack—or, for that matter, alcohol or the prescription sedatives and tranquilizers which constitute the largest part of the American drug problem in the late twentieth century. As post-hip editor Mark Satin wrote in 1989, "If the Sixties taught us anything, it is this: Drugs are neither good nor bad. When abused, they can cause great harm. When used properly, they can help us expand our consciousness and enjoy our world."[20]

Further, the hippies, were they here today, would point out that America has lost its perspective in the recent crusade against drugs, devoting enormous resources to fighting what is actually a small part of the national drug problem. By any standard the most problematic drug in the country is alcohol, which is used regularly by a substantial majority of adult Americans. According to one estimate made in 1989, alcohol costs the country over $116 billion per year (much of that in lost work time and decreased productivity), whereas illegal drugs cost society about half that—$60 billion or so. Alcohol kills an estimated 125,000 persons per year, while heroin and cocaine kill perhaps 6,000. (Tobacco dwarfs even alcohol here, with 390,000 deaths per year.)[21]

Finally, the hippies would raise the issue of the nature of the drug *problem*, saying that the *illegality* of drugs is the largest single component of what seems to be regarded today as a national crisis. The view of the majority of Americans, apparently, is that illicit drugs are wrong because they are illegal and that they can't be legalized because that would be capitulating to the enemy. That circular logic creates the kind of system in which a terribly destructive drug (alcohol) is legal while some drugs with little destructive potential (peyote, for example) are illegal. While certainly drug use would continue—and possibly increase somewhat—under legalization, much of what is regarded as destructive about drugs would be greatly diminished. The enormous profit potential of the drug trade would vanish with legalization, and with it the motivation for most of the violence spawned by drugs, which, after all, typically derives from disputes among sellers, not from use. Most hippies believed that legalization would do far more than the outlawing of drugs has to maintain social sanity, and there is little reason to think that they would believe otherwise today.

In the case of sex, it is plausible to believe that the sexual liberation of the hip era contributed to the worldwide epidemic of sexually transmitted diseases. Certainly the hippies were public and flamboyant in their pressing of the cause of a radical (by standards previously prevailing) ethics of sex; as American toleration of and participation in less strict sexual arrangements has spread, so have diseases. (Penicillin may have rendered some diseases unthreatening, but AIDS, herpes, and other stubborn ailments have raised the ante enormously.) One can argue that we are ethically obliged to keep our bodies as healthy as possible, and freewheeling sex does not seem to serve that cause. The hippies argued, however, that freedom and pleasure were key values in the new culture; would it not then be ethically permissible for one who engaged in sexual activity with eyes wide open to potential health risks to choose pleasure over health?

The arrival of AIDS would not affect the basic ethical equation. The stakes are higher for AIDS, obviously, than for other sexually transmitted diseases, and there can be little doubt that the presence of AIDS has transformed American sexual behavior. One's moral obligation to protect and inform one's partners becomes towering here, but the most basic ethical issue—is it right (or at least morally permissible) to have sex outside of heterosexual marriage?—is not changed by the advent of a new disease.

Certainly there are other seeming casualties of sexual freedom than disease. High divorce rates and great numbers of unwanted children born to single parents, for example, would seem to be sour fruits of freer sex. As with drugs, however, the hippies would argue, viewing the contemporary scene, that the countercultural message has been distorted and acted out irresponsibly. Freedom to engage in sexual activities once widely disapproved of does not mean that one is no longer responsible for one's actions. Using birth control and otherwise taking

responsibility for the consequences of one's actions were never condemned by the hippies.

✳ ✳ ✳ Did the Hippies Create a Disastrous Backlash?

One could argue that the hippies' net long-term accomplish-
ment was negative—that a backlash to hip excesses arose, boosting a
new conservatism that left the hip vision in the ashcan. After all, a
decade later there was a vocal, active New Right in America, a religio-
political movement that helped turn American politics in a profoundly
conservative direction. The rise of a New Right is a given; it is, however, difficult to figure out just how much of the social liberalization
so distasteful to the New Right came from the hippies and how much
came from other sources, such as New Deal liberalism.

The New Right has anathematized free sex, illegal drugs, secular
rock music, world peace through love and understanding, communal
sharing, and many other cherished hippie values. But the list of condemned liberalizations includes many more items than those especially
championed by the hippies. Jerry Falwell has been quoted as saying
that the largest single element in his own radicalization (if that can
possibly be the right term here), in which he moved from the traditional independent Baptist stance of rejecting and avoiding the corrupt secular world to advocacy of political involvement, was the Roe
vs. Wade Supreme Court decision affirming free choice on abortion.[22]
The hippies by and large did not condemn abortion, but they were
hardly major players on the pro-choice scene. They also were little involved in other causes which seemed to provoke the New Right, such
as the growth of the welfare state and the secularization of the public
schools.

The New Right arose as a backlash against half a century of liberalization of social mores and ideals; the hippies were a part of that
liberalization process, serving as highly visible agents for some of it.
They were certainly prominently in the public eye for several years,
and they aroused enormous animosity among some conservatives. To
the extent that they irritated the New Right, the hippies thus under-
mined their own goals. At this writing, however, the New Right seems
to be fading slightly; over the long run the verdict is not yet in.

✳ ✳ ✳ Outposts: Where Hip Still Survives

Perhaps the best place to see some survival for the counter-culture is in a few scattered enclaves. In some smaller cities, most of them college towns, and in quiet rural encampments life goes on. Not many would claim the title "hippie" today, but more than a few are still living the life.

The larger cities seem to have sheltered relatively few who continue to try to maintain hip ways. Perhaps the necessity for a substantial cash income and the ongoing degradation of urban life are among the causes of that. One still occasionally sees long hair, or sixties-style clothing, and surely the ingestion of psychoactive substances has not ceased. But cities are not great places for tuning in and dropping out.

Urban hip survival, such as it is, is probably best found in the booming New Age movement. *Movement* is an ambitious term here, because the New Age is utterly amorphous, and New Agers themselvers disagree enormously as to where to draw the boundary lines. Broadly, the movement involves mind and body, everything from massage to mental self-abnegation. Meditation, overtly religious or not, is part of the scene; so is a vast body of literature ranging from Theosophy to flying-saucer contactee testimonies. There are physical artifacts involved, such as crystals and runes; there is appreciation of old traditions in India, prechristian Europe, the Americas. New Age schools offer degrees and certificates in a myriad of fields from transpersonal psychology to water-witching. Transcending mundane reality is a common New Age theme, so psychological and spiritual programs and phenomena such as channeling proliferate. Defining and encompassing the New Age movement is impossible, but the movement is quite real and owes much to the hippies, those cultural revolutionaries who bucked tradition and explored the hidden fringes of contemporary life.

The hip subculture endures more identifiably in smaller places. Many college towns throughout the country have managed to accommodate persons who still live at least somewhat counterculturally. In those places, some children of hip have tried to work countercultural ideals into the social and physical fabric, as by operating businesses specializing in alternative energy or organic living, or by promoting community projects such as recycling and reducing use of automobiles. Persons with hip values have congregated in several such centers, particularly on the West Coast. One who visits the Oregon Country Fair or the Saturday Market in Eugene, for example, may well feel as if he or she were in the Haight-Ashbury, circa 1967.

The other locus of preservation of sixties idealism is the ongoing communitarian movement. Today they are usually called "intentional communities," not communes, but dozens, maybe hundreds, have survived from the hip era, and hundreds of new ones have been formed. Now as then no one is able to count the communities, but many are there, with a population perhaps in the tens of thousands. Some free-wheeling, secular communities have managed to overcome steep odds and keep themselves alive, even thriving; for example, Twin Oaks, near Louisa, Virginia, is nearing a quarter-century in age and has reportedly never been healthier.[23] Several religious communes have also survived; what is sometimes regarded as the archetypal hippie commune, the Farm community in Summertown, Tennessee, is still very much alive. Although enormous financial problems in the early 1980s led to an abandonment of important parts of the communal structure and to substantial depopulation, several hundreds of persons still live there, many of them continuing in their vows of poverty and community. The Farm still sponsors several projects that reflect classic hip idealism, such as Plenty, a foundation that does relief and development work in the United States and abroad, and the Natural Rights Center, a public-interest law firm that helps social outcasts and tilts at such formidable foes as the nuclear energy industry.

The gospel of alternative sexuality continues to be lived in some hip outposts. Perhaps the best example of that today is Kerista, a prosperous commune of several dozen members in the Haight-Ashbury that practices "polyfidelity," a system of shared partners in which one is to remain absolutely faithful to the group but, within the group, rotates among partners on a predetermined schedule.

So hip life goes on in a few enclaves; more significantly, it goes on in the lives of many who remain touched by the vision they experienced a generation ago. As one commented to me,

> I think our culture is in much better shape than it used to be. There is more diversity; things are more interesting. I am absolutely convinced that people accept one another more openly than they did before the hippies arrived; there is less prejudice in our

society than ever before. Sure, some hippies have become insurance salesmen, but none of them that I know deny that what they did was very good. I still believe the things I believed then. We all learned some things then that will be with us for the rest of our lives.[24]

Notes

CHAPTER 1. INTRODUCTION

1. J. L. Simmons and Barry Winograd, *It's Happening* (Santa Barbara: Marc-Laird Publications, 1966), 12–15.

2. William C. Shepherd, "Religion and the Counter Culture—A New Religiosity," *Sociological Inquiry* 42, no. 1 (1972): 7–8.

3. Chester Anderson, "God Works through Harry Anslinger," Los Angeles *Free Press*, 26 April 1968.

4. "Youth: The Hippies," *Time*, 7 July 1967, 20.

5. Ibid., 22.

6. Steven M. Tipton, *Getting Saved from the Sixties: Moral Meaning in Conversion and Cultural Change* (Berkeley: University of California Press, 1982), 14.

7. Theodore Roszak, *The Making of a Counter Culture* (Garden City, N.Y.: Doubleday, 1969).

8. John Gruen, *The New Bohemia* (New York: Grosset and Dunlap, 1966).

9. Norman Mailer, "The White Negro," in *Voices of Dissent* (New York: Grove, 1958), 199, 200, 206.

10. "The Declaration of Cultural Evolution," *East Village Other*, late May 1968 (illegible date). Authorship is not credited, but an earlier issue of *EVO* (about the middle of May—illegible date) stated that Leary, Ginsberg, Krassner, and Hoffman were working on the statement.

11. Art Johnston, "A Theory of Hip; Part One: 'What Have You Got?'" *Fifth Estate*, 15–30 November 1966.

12. Jean-Jacques Lebel, "Counter Culture: Hip Culture Ripped Off," *Spectator*, 8 December 1969.

13. Lawrence Lipton, "Radio Free America," Los Angeles *Free Press*, 3 May 1968.

14. Raymond Mungo, *Total Loss Farm: A Year in the Life* (New York: Dutton, 1970), 18.

15. Steve Haines, "To Build a Nation," Berkeley *Tribe*, 7–13 November 1969.

16. Walt Crowley, "Constipated Counter-Attack Catharsis," *Helix*, 19 September 1969.

17. Roszak, *Making of a Counter Culture*, 24.

18. Jack G. Burgess, "Notice to the Dead and Dying: You Are Standing on a Generation," Los Angeles *Free Press*, 25 April 1969.

19. George D. Maloney, "On Bridging the Generation Gap—Can We Work It Out?" Spokane *Natural*, 16–29 August 1968.

20. Andrew Kopkind, untitled article, *Rolling Stone*, 20 September 1969.

21. Laurence Leamer, *The Paper Revolutionaries: The Rise of the Underground Press* (New York: Simon and Schuster, 1972), chap. 4.

22. Paul Goodman, *New Reformation* (New York: Random House, 1970), chap. 4.

23. Richard Neville, *Play Power* (London: Jonathan Cape, 1970), 18.

24. Kenneth Westhues, using the term *counterculture* to comprehend any dissenting subculture, concluded from his research that "the most basic condition for the rise of a counterculture is perceived discrepancy between societal ideology and lived experience." See Kenneth Westhues, ed., *Society's Shadow: Studies in the Sociology of Countercultures* (Toronto: McGraw-Hill Ryerson, 1972), 141.

25. P. G. Stafford, "Acid, Rock and Revolution," *Seed* 2, no. 10 (1968).

26. Stan Iverson, "To Touch the Genitals," *Helix*, October 1968 (illegible date).

27. Quoted in Mayer Vishner, "Rock and Revolution," *Win*, 15 December 1968, 20–21.

28. Roszak, *Making of a Counter Culture*, 66.

29. Goodman, *New Reformation*, 202.

30. See Norman Mailer, *The Armies of the Night* (New York: New American Library, 1968).

31. "Changes" (a dialogue among Alan Watts, Timothy Leary, Allen Ginsberg, and Gary Snyder), San Francisco *Oracle* 1, no. 7 (1967). The specific quotation is attributed to Leary.

32. Mick Wheelock, "Is Love Dead?" Los Angeles *Free Press*, 22 November 1968.

33. Raymond Mungo, *Famous Long Ago: My Life and Hard Times with Liberation News Service* (Boston: Beacon, 1970), 53.

34. Ralph J. Gleason, "Perspectives: Is There a Death Wish in U.S.?" *Rolling Stone*, 5 April 1969.

35. Mungo, *Famous Long Ago*, 168.

36. Interview with Bob Maurice, *Great Speckled Bird*, 4 May 1970.

37. David Super-Straight, "Some Notes on the Violent Generation," Berkeley *Barb*, 1–7 August 1969.

38. Mungo, *Famous Long Ago*, 134–35.

39. Greil Marcus, "The Woodstock Festival," *Rolling Stone*, 20 September 1969.

40. Attributed to Bill Finn in "No Time for Sex," Berkeley *Barb*, 4 February 1965.

41. "Marxist Scholar Opines on Hips" (interview with George Novack of the Socialist Workers Party), Berkeley *Barb*, 12–18 May 1967.

42. "The Revolution Is Now!" Spokane *Natural*, 16–29 August 1968. Originally published in *Liberation*; distributed via Liberation News Service.

43. David McReynolds, "An Open Letter to: Richard Alpert," *Win*, July 1967, 10–12.

44. "Marcuse on the Hippie Revolution," Berkeley *Barb*, 4–10 August 1967.

45. Andrew Kimbrell, "The Coming Era of Activism: New Left Meets New Age," *Utne Reader* no. 26 (March/April 1988): 66.

46. "Warning to So-Called 'Paper Panthers,'" *Black Panther*, 14 September 1968, 10.

47. Harvey Cox, "God and the Hippies," *Playboy* 15, no. 1 (January 1968), 94.

48. Shepherd, "Religion and the Counter Culture," 3.

49. "'Clear Light' Sought for LSD Religionists," Berkeley *Barb*, 17 June 1966.

50. Ralph J. Gleason, "Perspectives: Are We Lost in a New Dark Age?" *Rolling Stone*, 13 December 1969.

51. "Headitorials," *Spectator*, 7 January 1969.

52. Steve Russell, "An Open Letter to the Kampus Krusade," *Rag*, 23 November 1970.

53. "Jesus Was a Militant," *Great Speckled Bird*, 2 February 1970.

54. Thaddeus Ashby and Rita Ashby, "Did Jesus Turn On?" Berkeley *Barb*, 23 December 1966.

55. Laurence Leamer argued that the underground press was the only "broad, unifying institution" the counterculture produced. See Leamer, *Paper Revolutionaries*, 13.

56. The three available collections are the Underground Press Collection (AMS Press), made available to member institutions by the Center for Re-

search Libraries in Chicago; a collection compiled and distributed by University Microfilms of Ann Arbor; and the Bell and Howell Underground Press Collection, which includes papers published in the years 1965 to 1970, the years during which the underground press rose and flourished.

57. Abe Peck, *Uncovering the Sixties: The Life and Times of the Underground Press* (New York: Pantheon, 1985), xiv–xv.

CHAPTER 2. THE ETHICS OF DOPE

1. Tom Coffin, "Dope," *Great Speckled Bird*, 6 October 1969.

2. "Dope Summit Conference," *Dallas Notes*, 2–15 April 1969.

3. Quoted in Norman Hartweg, "Psychedelic Prophet Alpert to Speak in Los Angeles," Los Angeles *Free Press*, 3 September 1965.

4. Jan Hodenfield, "It Was Like Balling for the First Time," *Rolling Stone*, 20 September 1969.

5. Mungo, *Total Loss Farm*, 71.

6. "Dr. Timothy Leary" (excerpts from a debate at the University of Utah), *Electric Newspaper* 1, no. 2 (1968).

7. "Psychiatrist Says Teens Who Don't Smoke Pot Are 'Sick,'" *Hips Voice*, 15 April 1970.

8. "Poll Indicates 69% Have Used Grass," *University Daily Kansan*, 8 October 1971.

9. Cited in Peter Stafford, ed., *Psychedelic Baby Reaches Puberty* (New York: Praeger, 1971), 27.

10. "Drug Use Not Abating, Study Shows" (National College Poll), Lawrence *Daily Journal-World*, 15 November 1972.

11. *Marihuana: A Signal of Misunderstanding* (Official Report of the National Commission on Marihuana and Drug Abuse) (New York: New American Library, 1972), 39.

12. Lewis Yablonsky, *The Hippie Trip* (New York: Pegasus, 1968), 346–47.

13. According to one report, marijuana arrests increased from 6,800 in 1963 to 23,952 in 1966; the amount of marijuana seized by border officials increased from 6,444 pounds to 23,716 pounds during the same period. Source: FBI crime reports, cited in "Bust Measurements," *The Marijuana Review*, October–December 1969.

14. Jan Hodenfield, "It Was Like Balling for the First Time," *Rolling Stone*, 20 September 1969.

15. "Intergalactic Union Dopogram," *East Village Other*, 11 August 1970. Originally published in *Scanlan's*, August 1970.

16. "Vice-President's Daughter Caught with Marijuana," Los Angeles *Free Press*, 5 September 1969.

17. *Marihuana: A Signal of Misunderstanding*, 38.

18. Helen Swick Perry, *The Human Be-In* (New York: Basic Books, 1970), 73.

19. Hal Cromley, quoted in Ben Fong-Torres, "Feds' Dope Circus: 'How Much LSD Do You Take to Be Addicted?'" *Rolling Stone*, 29 November 1969.

20. "Pot Conference in Buffalo," *East Village Other*, 14 March 1969.

21. Attributed to Phil Melman in Robert Novick, "Phil Melman Busted at 75," San Francisco *Express-Times*, 7 March 1968 (via Liberation News Service).

22. Mike Scudder, "High School Drugs," *Buffalo Chip*, November 1968.

23. "Shit as a Household Word," Berkeley *Barb*, 19–25 September 1969.

24. The Rev. Stanley J. Keach, "Thoughts on the Drug Scene," *Speak Easy* 1, no. 6 (1968).

25. Tom Coffin, "Everybody's Talkin'," *Great Speckled Bird*, 22 September 1969. On this point see also Timothy Miller, "Drug Bust in Kansas," *Christian Century* 88, no. 11 (17 March 1971): 332–33.

26. "Leary and Alpert: Turn On/Tune In/Drop Out," Berkeley *Barb*, 24 June 1966.

27. Ken Anderson, "Dope," *Hartford's Other Voice*, 25 September 1969.

28. "Heads Revolting," interview with Art Kleps, Berkeley *Barb*, 20–26 December 1968. (Originally published in *Real Free Press*.)

29. [Stephen Gaskin], *Hey Beatnik! This Is the Farm Book* (Summertown, Tenn.: The Book Publishing Co., 1974), unpaginated.

30. Allen Ginsberg, "The Great Marijuana Hoax," *Atlantic Monthly* 218, no. 5 (November 1966). Reprinted in the *Electric Newspaper* 1 no. 2 (1968).

31. Ronald Broudy, "Don't Legalize Pot," *Rat*, 19–30 April 1968.

32. Howard Moody, "Heroin: The Law Is Worse than the Drug," *Village Voice*, 14 September 1972.

33. Ralph Metzner saw two common elements in all the dope churches: the need on the part of many individuals to structure the dope experience on the assumption that structured and/or ritualized use of dope produced a better experience, and the need to provide social self-protection in a fashion similar to that of a labor union. ("An Interview with Ralph Metzner," *Seed*, 11–25 August 1967.)

34. Richard Alpert, (illegible title), San Francisco *Oracle*, January 1967.

35. Interview with Timothy Leary, *Yarrowstalks* oo, no. 1 (1967).

36. Timothy Leary, "Head Line," *Rag*, 9 January 1967. (Originally published in the San Francisco *Oracle*.)

37. Timothy Leary, "The Politics, Ethics, and Meaning of Marijuana," in David Solomon, ed., *The Marihuana Papers* (New York: New American Library, 1966), 130.

38. Timothy Leary, *High Priest* (New York: World, 1968), flyleaf.

39. Timothy Leary, "Head Line," *Rag*, 9 January 1967. (Originally published in the San Francisco *Oracle*.)

40. Art Kleps (interviewed by Joe Dana), "The New Gurus," *Oracle of Southern California*, December 1967.

41. Peter Novick, "Underground God," Washington *Free Press*, 19 March 1968.

42. "Heads Revolting," Berkeley *Barb*, 20–26 December 1968. (Originally published in the *Real Free Press*.)

43. Art Kleps, *The Boo Hoo Bible* (San Cristobal, N.M.: Toad Press, 1971).

44. Art Grosman, "Interview with a 66 Year Old Peyote Eater," Washington *Free Press*, 16–30 July 1968.

45. For the Shiva Fellowship Church, see "A Temple of Cannabis," *Rolling Stone*, 1 November 1969; for the Psychedelic Venus Church, see "Sex Drug Cult," Berkeley *Tribe*, 27 November–5 December 1969; for the Fellowship of the Clear Light, see "Clear Light not Bright," Berkeley *Barb*, 8 July 1966; for the American Council of Internal Divinity, see "The Gossiping Guru," San Francisco *Oracle* 1, no. 6 (1967); for the Psychedelic Peace Fellowship, see "Psychedelic Peace Fellowship," *Oracle of Southern California*, October 1967.

46. Michael Kindman, "On This Cube I Will Build My Church," *Fifth Estate*, 1-15 January 1967.

47. "Intergalactic Union Dopogram," *East Village Other*, 11 August 1970. (Originally published in *Scanlan's*, August 1970).

48. "Leary and Alpert: Turn On/Tune In/Drop Out," Berkeley *Barb*, 24 June 1966.

49. Tuli Kupferberg, "The Hip and the Square," Berkeley *Barb*, 4–10 August 1967.

50. Will Albert, "Who Is Mary Jane?" *Notes from the Underground*, 15–31 August 1967. (Originally published in *The Paper*.)

51. Timothy Leary offered this definition of the religious experience: "The religious experience is the ecstatic, incontrovertibly certain, subjective discovery of answers to four basic spiritual questions," which are the Ultimate-Power question ("What is the Ultimate Power [or] Basic Energy which moves the universe, creates life? What is the cosmic plan?"), the Life question ("What is life, where did it start, where is it going?"), the Human-Destiny question ("What is man, whence did he come, and where is he going?"), and the Ego question ("What am I? What is my place in the plan?"). See Timothy Leary, "The Religious Experience: Its Production and Interpretation," *Journal of Psychedelic Drugs* 1, no. 2 (Winter 1967): 7.

52. "Windcatcher," *Good Times*, 7 August 1969.

53. "Sacraments are catalysts rather than ends. Anything one gets from the marijuana experience was there all the time, only perhaps unexplored." Will Albert, "Who Is Mary Jane?" *Notes from the Underground*, 15–31 August 1967. (Originally published in *The Paper*.)

54. "Start Your Own Religion," *Oracle of Southern California*, June 1967.

55. Mel Lyman, "To All Who Would Know," *Seed* 2, no. 1 (1968). (Originally published in the *Avatar*.)

56. "Black Market Research," *Notes on Pot (Dallas Notes)*, 16–29 February 1968; "Dope Quiz Results," *Fifth Estate*, 1–15 April 1968.

57. Paul Krassner (interview), "LSD, Revolution and God," San Francisco *Oracle* 1, no. 6 (1967).

58. Tom Wolfe, *The Electric Kool-Aid Acid Test* (New York: Farrar, Straus and Giroux, 1968), 234.

59. Leary, "The Religious Experience: Its Production and Interpretation," 6.

60. R. E. L. Masters and Jean Houston, *The Varieties of Psychedelic Experience* (New York: Dell, 1966), 265.

61. Walter Houston Clark, *Chemical Ecstasy* (New York: Sheed and Ward, 1969), 62.

62. "The Attractions of LSD," Washington *Free Press*, 7 March 1968.

63. Walter N. Pahnke, "Drugs and Mysticism: An Analysis of the Relationship between Psychedelic Drugs and the Mystical Consciousness," Ph.D. dissertation, Harvard University, 1963.

64. "Bishop Pike: Interview," *Helix*, 29 September 1967. In a similar vein, Walter Houston Clark has written that drugs are "always a factor" in religious experience "if we could admit as 'drugs' those powerful biochemicals, more often called hormones, which are natural in the human body and without whose involvement no act of human consciousness, sacred or profane, can occur." Clark, *Chemical Ecstasy*, 7–8.

65. Allen H. Reid, "An Open Letter on Drugs to Swami Satchidananda," *Hips Voice*, 26 August 1970. Reid is replying to the Swami's contention that drugs cannot be a way to true mystical insight.

66. "Why Psychedelics?" *Oracle of Southern California*, August 1967.

67. P. G. Stafford, "Acid Rock and Revolution," *Seed* 2, no. 10 (1968).

68. Shepherd, "Religion and the Counter Culture," 6.

69. "Shiva Missionary and Cop Go Up in Cloud of Smoke," Berkeley *Barb*, 14–20 June 1968.

70. "The Noblest of All Human Professions: Clear Light," Berkeley *Barb*, 18–24 December 1970. (Originally published in *Georgia Straight*.)

71. "Shit as a Household Word," Berkeley *Barb*, 19–25 September 1969.

72. "Intergalactic Union Dopogram," *East Village Other*, 11 August 1970. (Originally published in *Scanlan's*, August 1970).

73. P. G. Stafford, "Acid Rock and Revolution—Part II," *Seed* 2, no. 11 (1968).

74. R. Gordon Wasson has established that the *soma* of ancient India was the *Amanita Muscaria*, a psychoactive mushroom. (See R. Gordon Wasson, *Soma: Divine Mushroom of Immortality* [New York: Harcourt, Brace and World, 1969].) The same mushroom may have been a key ingredient in the Elusinian mysteries, one of the forerunners of contemporary secret societies. (See Masters and Houston, *Varieties of Psychedelic Experience*, 251.)

75. Thaddeus and Rita Ashby, "Did Jesus Turn On?" Berkeley *Barb*, December 23, 1966.

76. John Allegro, *The Sacred Mushroom and the Cross* (London: Hodder and Stoughton, 1970), p. xx.

77. Gridley Wright, "Strawberry Fields Forever . . . ?" *Oracle of Southern California*, August, 1967.

78. Paul Scorpio, "LSD and Me (Part III)," *Distant Drummer*, 26 March 1970.

79. Timothy Leary, "Playboy Interview," *Playboy* 13, no. 9 (September 1966). Reprinted in the Los Angeles *Free Press*, 1–7 September 1967.

80. "Black Market Research," *Notes on Pot (Dallas Notes)*, 16–29 February 1968; "Dope Quiz Results," *Fifth Estate*, 1–15 April 1968.

81. "Aquarius, M. D.," *Great Speckled Bird*. 3 November 1969.

82. William Braden, *The Age of Aquarius* (Cleveland: Quadrangle Books, 1970), 237–47. This thesis is also supported by Philip Slater, *The Pursuit of Loneliness: American Culture at the Breaking Point* (Boston: Beacon, 1970), chap. 1.

83. Alex Forman and F. P. Salstrom, "Revolution, Diggers Style," *Distant Drummer*, 3–10 October 1969.

84. "Tompkin Square Smoke-In," *East Village Other*, 5–17 August 1967.

85. Claudia McCarthy, "A Search for Self," *Old Mole*, 29 May–11 June 1970.

86. Walt Crowley, "Those Vegematic Blues," *Helix*, 30 April 1970.

87. Andrew Weil, *The Natural Mind* (Boston: Houghton Mifflin, 1972), 96–97.

88. Timothy Leary, Introduction to David Solomon, ed., *LSD: The Consciousness-Expanding Drug* (New York: G. P. Putnam's Sons, 1964), 18–21.

89. Timothy Leary, Ralph Metzner, and Richard Alpert, *The Psychedelic Experience* (New Hyde Park, N.Y.: University Books, 1964), 11.

90. Ibid.

91. "Shit as a Household Word," Berkeley *Barb*, 19–25 September 1969.

92. Jean Raisler, "Placid on Acid," Berkeley *Tribe*, 29 August–4 September 1969.

93. "Black Market Research," *Notes on Pot (Dallas Notes)*, 16–29 February 1968; "Dope Quiz Results," *Fifth Estate*, 1–15 April 1968.

94. John Rosevear, "Dope Smoking—The State of the Art," Los Angeles *Free Press*, 14 June 1968.

95. According to Howard Moody, a Massachusetts court once held that alcohol relieved tension and was otherwise beneficial in effect, but that marijuana could only be used for pleasure and could therefore constitutionally be outlawed. In effect, the court said that pleasure equalled abuse in the realm of drugs. See Moody, "Heroin," 20.

96. "Black Market Research," *Notes on Pot (Dallas Notes)*, 16–29 February 1968.

97. See, for example, the statement of Dr. Bernard Rascombe, "Psychiatrist Says Teens Who Don't Smoke Pot Are 'Sick,'" *Hips Voice*, 15 April 1970.

98. Eugene Schoenfeld, M.D., "Does LSD Really Harm?" *Florida Free Press*, 30 June 1968.

99. Thane Gower Ritalin, "The Hippies and the Hypocrites," *Seed*, 11–25 August 1967.

100. Many scholarly books and articles on the medical applications of marijuana and LSD have appeared since the late 1950s. One important work on the medical uses of LSD is H. A. Abramson, ed., *The Use of LSD in Psychotherapy and Alcoholism* (Indianapolis: Bobbs-Merrill, 1967). See also Albert A. Kurland, M.D., "The Therapeutic Potential of LSD in Medicine," in Richard C. DeBold and Russell C. Leaf, eds., *LSD, Man and Society* (Middletown, Conn.: Wesleyan University Press, 1967).

101. See, for example, Robert Novick, "Phil Melman Busted at 75," San Francisco *Express-Times*, 7 March 1968 (via Liberation News Service); "The Attractions of LSD," Washington *Free Press*, 7 March 1968.

102. "Marijuana as Medicine," Los Angeles *Free Press*, 20 March 1970 (via Liberation News Service).

103. "Black Market Research," *Notes on Pot* (*Dallas Notes*), 16–29 February 1968; "Dope Quiz Results," *Fifth Estate*, 1–15 April 1968.

104. Ginsberg, "The Great Marijuana Hoax," as reprinted in the *Electric Newspaper* 1, no. 2 (1968).

105. Lawrence Lipton, "The High Priest of LSD," Los Angeles *Free Press*, 4 October 1968. (Originally published in *Paris Review*.)

106. Lois Lane, "Leary Love Rap," interview, Berkeley *Barb*, 26 December 1969–2 January 1970.

107. David Faber, "Smack Down," *Argus*, 9–23 February 1970.

108. Robert Claiborne, "Buying Time and Safety: Let's Legalize Heroin," *Village Voice*, 16 December 1971.

109. Allen Ginsberg, "Mafia and Junk," Los Angeles *Free Press*, 22 May 1970. (Originally published in *Good Times*.)

110. "Leary Speed Warning," *Kaleidoscope*, 13–26 February 1970.

111. "Allen Ginsberg on Speed, Etc.," *Distant Drummer* 1, no. 9 (1968). (Originally published in the *Electric Newspaper*.)

112. David Faber, "Smack Down," *Argus*, 9–23 February 1970.

113. *Dallas Notes*, 15 October–4 November 1969.

114. "Peanut Butter Spreads," Spokane *Natural*, 7–20 November 1969.

115. "I Saw the Best Minds of My Generation," interview with Allen Ginsberg, *East Village Other*, 14 March 1969.

116. "Aquarius M.D.," *Great Speckled Bird*, 22 September 1969.

117. Tom Coffin, "Everybody's Talkin'," *Great Speckled Bird*, 22 September 1969.

118. In 1989 Kesey said, "I never dosed anybody. I never gave anybody drugs without telling him. It's rape. You can't violate a person like that. I have been dosed by people trying to impress me. I can't tell you how much I hate it." See John Lehndorff, "Kesey Takes in Life with a 60's Slant," Wichita *Eagle*, 17 September 1989, p. 2E.

119. Timothy Leary, "Dope," *Electric Newspaper* 1, no. 3 (1968).

120. Art Kunkin, "A Personal Statement by the Publisher on Acid Testing," Los Angeles *Free Press*, 11 April 1969.

121. Allen Ginsberg, "Renaissance or Die," San Francisco *Oracle*, January 1967.

122. See Ed Sanders, *The Family* (New York: Dutton, 1970).

123. Lawrence Lipton, "Radio Free America," Los Angeles *Free Press*, 16 January 1970.

124. Dr. David E. Smith, "Life with Manson," Berkeley *Barb*, 16–22 January 1970.

125. Sanders, *The Family*, 69ff. Sanders dealt especially with the Process Church of the Final Judgment ("an English occult society dedicated to observing and aiding the end of the world by stirring up murder, violence and chaos, and dedicated to the proposition that they, the Process, shall survive the gore as the chosen people") as the largest and most dangerous offender; his criticisms were sufficiently incisive (and insufficiently substantiated) that under the threat of a lawsuit he dropped the material from his "revised" paperback edition. However, many years later he was still privately claiming that his charges were entirely true (personal communication).

126. Untitled statement by Mel Lyman, *American Avatar* (undated), 1969.

127. David Felton, "The Lyman Family's Holy Siege of America," *Rolling Stone*, 23 December 1971 and 6 January 1972.

128. Lucian K. Truscott IV, "Chop, Chop: Age of Psychedelic Fascism," *Village Voice*, 14 October 1971.

129. Bruce Hoffman, "Yogi Hits Weed for Binding Users to 'Valley of Illusions,'" Los Angeles *Free Press*, 3 October 1969.

130. Allan Cohen, quoted in "Meher Baba Tells It," *Screw*, 1 January 1969. (Originally published in *Oz*.)

131. Allen H. Reid, "An Open Letter on Drugs to Swami Satchidananda," *Hips Voice*, 26 August 1970.

132. Allen Ginsberg, "Allen and the Maharishi," *Florida Free Press*, 30 June 1968. (Originally published in the San Francisco *Express-Times*.)

133. Bill Drew and Mike Rosen, "Waukegan Kids," *Connections*, 11 December 1968–15 January 1969.

134. "The Revolution Is Now!" Spokane *Natural*, 16–29 August 1968. (Originally published in *Liberation*; distributed by Liberation News Service.)

135. "David Crosby of the Byrds," *Oracle of Southern California*, October 1967.

136. Ron Norman, "An Open Letter from One Hippie," *Seventy-Nine Cent Spread*, 5 November 1968.

137. David Faber, "Smack Down," *Argus*, 9–23 February 1970.

138. "Mike Curb and Richard Nixon Battle Dopers," *Rolling Stone*, 26 November 1970.

1. The National Organization for Women was formed in 1966; most other new feminist groups were formed in 1968 or thereafter. The major books that defined the movement were almost all published in 1970 or later. See Lois W. Banner, *Women in Modern America: A Brief History* (San Diego: Harcourt Brace Jovanovich, 2nd ed., 1984), 254–55.

2. John Cunnick, "Dump Truck Baby," *Helix*, 2 November 1967.

3. Paul Goodman, "The New Reformation," *New York Times Magazine*, 14 September 1969, p. 147.

4. Leah Fritz, "Female Sexuality and the Liberated Orgasm," Berkeley *Tribe*, 16–23 October 1970.

5. Albert Ellis saw several correlations between activism and liberated sexuality. See Albert Ellis, "Sex and Revolution: How Are They Related?" *Other Scenes*, August 1970.

6. "In Search of the Erotic," *Good Times*, 4 December 1970.

7. Dave Wilson, "Scaramouche," *Haight-Ashbury Maverick* 1, no. 4 (1968). (Originally published in *Avatar*.)

8. "Sex in Spokane," Spokane *Natural*, 8 December 1967.

9. Don H. Somerville, "Sexology," *Helix* 9, no. 9 (1969).

10. Colleen Houlihan, "A Chick on Sex," *Walrus* 2, no. 4 (1968).

11. "On 'n' Off on Zensible Sex," Berkeley *Barb*, 18 March 1966.

12. See P. N. Dedeaux, "Sade Lib," *Village Voice*, 13 May 1971; Terry Kolb, "Masochist's Lib," *Village Voice*, 13 May 1971; Harold Nederland, "Asexuals Have Problems Too," *Village Voice*, 25 February 1971; Howard Smith, "Scenes," *Village Voice*, 22 April 1971.

13. "Very Pleasurable Politics," *Rat*, 17 December 1970–6 January 1971.

14. Dave Wilson, "Scaramouche," *Haight-Ashbury Maverick* 1, no. 4 (1968). (Originally published in *Avatar*.)

15. See, for example, "Gentlemen . . . The Queen," Berkeley *Barb*, 10–16 May 1968.

16. One underground writer told of a game called S.E.X. which was being sold in Berkeley—"a total non-stop adult sex game where two, three, or four couples roll the dice to determine who does what to who. S.E.X. takes over where strip poker left off." See John Wilcock, "Other Scenes," Berkeley *Barb*, 5–11 December 1969.

17. About the only sexual preferences that were questioned even occasionally in the hip world were pornography and sexual devices, such as dildoes. One writer contended, "Sexual liberation is not achieved with gadgets and machines that temporarily eliminate the boredom of conventional sexuality. Fuck books or orgy movies will not teach us to relate to one another in a new, equal, giving, non-possessive manner." Pam Gwin, "Buy, Sell, Don't Smell," *Great Speckled Bird*, 15 December 1969.

18. Bob Cummings, "Total Sexuality," *Rag*, 19 June 1969. (Originally published in *Modern Utopian*.)

19. Don H. Somerville, "Sexology," *Helix* 9, no. 4 (1969).

20. See Allan D. Coult, Ph.D., "Sex, Religion, and LSD," *Oracle of Southern California*, January 1968.

21. The most comprehensive case for an ethics of homosexuality was "A Gay Manifesto," written by Carl Wittman. See Los Angeles *Free Press*, 14 August 1970. This manifesto was widely reprinted in the underground press.

22. Dan Borroff, "Gay Is Beautiful," *Hips Voice*, 27 May 1970. (Originally published in *Seed*.)

23. Ellen Breiter, "In Ancient Greece You Were 'Queer' If You Weren't Homosexual," *Williamette Bridge*, 29 May–4 June 1970.

24. "Gay Lib," *Argus* 2, no. 5 (1970). (Originally published in *Rat*.)

25. Jefferson Poland, "So Try It!!!" Berkeley *Barb*, 19–25 June 1970.

26. The Sandman, "Get Gay!!" Berkeley *Tribe*, 20 October–6 November 1970.

27. Carl Wittman, "A Gay Manifesto," Los Angeles *Free Press*, 14 August 1970.

28. Bill Wingell, "A Time for Holding Hands," *Distant Drummer*, 10 July 1969.

29. Don Jackson, "Brother Don Has a Dream," Los Angeles *Free Press*, 14 August 1970.

30. Many also advocated legislation permitting homosexual marriages. Such marriages did occur publicly at least by 1969, although of course they did not have the sanction of the state. See "Wedding Rights," Berkeley *Barb*, 18–24 April 1969.

31. Leo E. Laurence, "Gay Page," Berkeley *Tribe*, 21–28 November 1969.

32. T. R. Wayne-Hill, "Houston Homosexual Speaks Out," *Space City News*, 11–25 October 1969.

33. Quoted in "Mattachine International," *Great Speckled Bird*, 6 October 1969.

34. T. R. Wayne-Hill, "Houston Homosexual Speaks Out," *Space City News*, 11–25 October 1969.

35. "Gay Revolution Comes Out," *Rat*, 12–26 August 1969.

36. "Beast and the Beauty," *Helix*, 18 July 1968.

37. LeRoy Moore, Jr., "From Profane to Sacred America," *Journal of the American Academy of Religion* 39, no. 3 (September 1971): 333.

38. *Ibid.*

39. Gina Shepard, "If It's Their Thing Just Let 'em Leer," Berkeley *Barb*, 7–13 July 1967.

40. Michael Stanley, "Let It All Hang Out," Los Angeles *Free Press*, 11 October 1968.

41. See, for example, "Fun-A-Nude," *Kaleidoscope*, 7–20 June 1968; "Campus Nudity," *Helix* 7, no. 10 (1969).

42. Neville, *Play Power*, 80.

43. Michael Stanley, "Let It All Hang Out," Los Angeles *Free Press*, 11 October 1968.

44. "What's Nudes?" Spokane *Natural*, 28 February–13 March 1969 (via Liberation News Service). This incident, with an accompanying explicit photograph, was widely reported in the underground press.

45. Sue Marshall, "Pot-Sex Church Celebrates Hedonism," Los Angeles *Free Press*, 13 March 1970.

46. "Sex is not practiced religiously. It is more of a happening." Yablonsky, *Hippie Trip*, 23.

47. Gina Shepard, "If It's Their Thing Just Let 'em Leer," Berkeley *Barb*, 7–13 July 1967.

48. "The Om United Nude Brigade," *Rolling Stone*, 23 July 1970.

49. Phil Pukas, "Omigod," Berkeley *Barb*, 12–18 June 1970.

50. "OMM," Berkeley *Barb*, 5–11 June 1970.

51. "Guru Ginsberg's Little Homilies on Holy Nudity," Berkeley *Barb*, 14–20 June 1968.

52. Sue Marshall, "Pot-Sex Church Celebrates Hedonism," Los Angeles *Free Press*, 13 March 1970.

53. Leo Laurence, "Doin' It on the Altar," Berkeley *Tribe*, 2–9 January 1970. Some Gay Liberation Front members were upset by the publication of this description, since it represented an attitude not all of them shared. See Leo E. Laurence, "Gay God Squad," Berkeley *Tribe*, 9–15 January 1970.

54. Venereal diseases were on a sharp upward curve during the hip era. In 1955 362,502 cases were reported; that figure jumped to 628,812 in 1969, and to 693,606 in 1970. Although the number of cases of syphilis declined greatly with the advent of antibiotic drugs, the incidence of gonorrhea, the most common sexually transmitted disease in hippie days, increased even more sharply. See the *Statistical Abstract of the United States, 1972* 93rd ed. (Washington: Bureau of the Census, 1972), 77.

55. Dov Witz, "Don't Applaud the Clap—or—You Only Hurt the One You Love," *Seed* 1, no. 7 (1967).

56. Rick Strauss, "The Clap," *Oracle of Southern California*, August 1967.

57. Dave Wilson, "Scaramouche," *Haight-Ashbury Maverick* 1, no. 4 (1968). (Originally published in the *Avatar*.)

58. Interview with Timothy Leary, *Yarrowstalks* oo, no. 1 (1967).

59. See, for example, Kristal Higrass, "Choosing a Method," *Seed* 2, no. 9 (1968).

60. Twig Daniels, "Abortion!" *Buffalo Chip*, December 1968.

61. Mary Hamilton, "Survival in the Jungle—Number Eight," *Rat*, 10–23 September 1969.

62. Women's Liberation Health Collective, "Women, Abortion, and Health Care," *Rat*, 25 December 1969–7 January 1970.

63. Paul Krassner and Ken Kesey, "An Impolite Interview with Ken Kesey," *The Realist* no. 90 (May–June 1971): 47.

64. [Gaskin], *Hey Beatnik!*, unpaginated.

65. "Hooray for Orgies," Berkeley *Barb*, 13 May 1966.

66. "Sex Freedom League Aims Clarified," Berkeley *Barb*, 15 April 1966.

67. "More Nude Happenings for Berkeley," Berkeley *Barb*, 25 February 1966.

68. "'Enjoy, Enjoy' Sex Duet's Spring Tune," Berkeley *Barb*, 22 April 1966.

69. Leo E. Laurence, "SFL—Not Just Fucking Around," Berkeley *Tribe*, 29 August–4 September 1969.

70. Jaakov Kohn, "Interview with Tim Leary," *Rag*, 12 June 1969. (Originally published in the *East Village Other*.)

71. Quoted in "SCUM Manifesto," *Connections*, 5–20 February 1969.

72. Judith Brown, "Women's Liberation," *Great Speckled Bird*, 11 November 1968. (Originally published in the *Southern Patriot*.)

73. Vivian Estellachild, "Hippie Communes," *Women: A Journal of Liberation* 2, no. 2 (1970): 40–41.

74. Tiresias, "A Kiss on the Mouth," Berkeley *Barb*, 23–29 January 1970.

75. Martha Shelley, "Stepin Fetchit Woman," *Seed* 5, no. 2 (1970).

76. Peggy Persephone and Robin of Arc, "Witch Power," *Rat*, 15–28 November 1968.

77. *Ibid.*

78. Sherrie Rubin, "Hymens for Husbands," *Everywoman*, 19 June 1970.

79. Marion Meade, "Women and Rock: Sexism Set to Music," *Women: A Journal of Liberation* (Fall 1970): 24–26.

80. "Women Take Over Rat," *Rat*, 6–23 February 1970.

81. Peck, *Uncovering the Sixties*, 213.

82. Robin Morgan, "Goodbye to All That," *Rat*, 6–23 February 1970.

83. Jefferson Fuck Poland, "Is Berkeley Fucking?" Berkeley *Barb*, 10–16 April 1970.

84. Tom Hayden, "Tom Objects," Berkeley *Barb*, 18–24 October 1968.

85. Bill Stanley, "The Pseudo-Sexual Revolution," *Walrus*, 1 March 1970.

CHAPTER 4. THE ETHICS OF ROCK

1. Chester Anderson, "Notes from the New Geology," San Francisco *Oracle* 1, no. 6 (1967).

2. Geoffrey Stokes, "The Sixties," in Ed Ward, Geoffrey Stokes, and Ken Tucker, *Rock of Ages: The Rolling Stone History of Rock and Roll* (New York: Summit Books/Simon and Schuster, 1986), 252.

3. Ron Jarvis, "When the Mode of the Music Changes," *Space City!* 17–30 January 1970.

4. John Sinclair, "Rock and Roll Dope," *Fifth Estate*, 4–18 June 1968.

5. John Sinclair, "Rock and Roll Dope," *Fifth Estate*, 28 November–11 December 1968.

6. Bill Kerby, "Pop: Toward a New Theatre," Los Angeles *Free Press*, 20 October 1967. "It really isn't a very good idea to abstract rock lyrics from the accompanying music for isolated scrutiny. Rock is essentially an appeal to the gut sense of rhythm, intensely energy-releasing and sexual. In this respect rock magnifies the condition of all poetry." (Karen Murphy and Ronald Gross, "All You Need Is Love. Love Is All You Need," in David Manning White, ed., *Pop Culture in America* [Chicago: Quadrangle, 1970], 206.)

7. John Sinclair, "Rock & Roll Dope," *Fifth Estate*, 4–18 June 1968.

8. Chester Anderson, "Notes from the New Geology," San Francisco *Oracle* 1, no. 6 (1967).

9. Jon Landau, "Rock 1970," *Rolling Stone*, 2 December 1970.

10. Generally, the counterculture's position on rock technology reflects its position on technology as a whole. Steve Levine, an editor of the San Francisco *Oracle*, was asked by Leonard and Deborah Wolf how the counterculture could reconcile its objections to technology with the necessity of technology for rock. His response was that the objection was never so much to the technology itself as to its uses. (See Leonard Wolf, ed., *Voices from the Love Generation* [Boston: Little, Brown, 1968], 55.)

11. Charles Reich, *The Greening of America* (New York: Random House, 1970), 245.

12. Quoted in Jack Hutton, "The Rolling Stone Interview: Ringo," *Rolling Stone*, 10 February 1968.

13. P. G. Stafford, "Acid Rock and Revolution—Part II," *Seed* 2, no. 11 (1968).

14. Ron Jarvis, "When the Mode of the Music Changes," *Space City!*, 17–30 January 1970. MC5, incidentally, eventually reversed its stand and bowed out of revolutionary rock.

15. Jonathan Eisen, quoted in Joseph Ferrandino, "Rock Culture and the Development of Social Consciousness," in William Slate, ed., *Power to the People: New Left Writings* (New York: Tower, 1970), 177.

16. Interview with Country Joe McDonald, *Good Times*, 23 October 1969.

17. Unsigned letter to the editor, *Rag*, 12 October 1970.

18. Plato, *Republic*, Book III, 401 (my translation).

19. Ralph J. Gleason, "Songs Would Do More Than Books," *Rolling Stone*, 1 March 1969.

20. Ralph J. Gleason, "Festival Paranoia," *Rolling Stone*, 6 September 1969.

21. Ralph J. Gleason, "Fighting Fire with Fire: An End to Logic," *Rolling Stone*, 28 May 1970.

22. Ellen Sander, "Dear Abbie," Los Angeles *Free Press*, 5 September 1969.

23. Arthur Johnson, "Music as God," *Distant Drummer*, 12–25 December 1968.

24. Irwin Silber, "The Topical Song 'Revolution' and How It Fizzled Out," *Heterodoxical Voice*, November 1968. (Originally published in the *Guardian*.)

25. Edward Taub, "A Heavyweight Fades," *North Carolina Anvil*, 18 July 1970.

26. Simmons and Winograd, *It's Happening*, 158.

27. James T. Carey, "The Ideology in Popular Lyrics: A Content Analysis," in Westhues, *Society's Shadow*, 99.

28. *Ibid.*, 109.

29. "Violence, Psychedelics, and Cultural Revolution—Now," *Rag*, 3 July 1969. (Originally published in *Georgia Straight*.)

30. Ralph J. Gleason, "Bob Dylan and the Children's Crusade," in *Ramparts* editors, eds., *Conversations with the New Reality* (San Francisco: Canfield Press, 1971), 72.

31. "The Rolling Stone Interview: Bob Dylan," *Rolling Stone*, 20 January 1968.

32. Jonathan Cott, "The Rolling Stone Interview: John Lennon," *Rolling Stone*, 23 November 1968.

33. John Vicente, "A Beatle Meets the Press" (George Harrison interview), *Oracle of Southern California*, August 1967.

34. Jon Landau, "Rock 1970," *Rolling Stone*, 2 December 1970.

35. David Satterfield, "Country Music in America (Part I)," *Spectator*, 11 November 1969.

36. "Rock Rip-Off," *Seed* 4, no. 10 (1969).

37. Thorne Dreyer, "Love and Haight," *Rag*, 5 June 1967.

38. Henry P. Dankowski, "Beggars' Banquet," Berkeley *Tribe*, 12–19 December 1969.

39. "The View from the Mud," *Rolling Stone*, 6 August 1970.

40. Gary Thiher, "Woodstock: Escape from Amerika," *Rag* 3, no. 28 (1969).

41. Max Lerner, quoted by Jan Hodenfield, "It Was Like Balling for the First Time," *Rolling Stone*, 20 September 1969.

42. Greil Marcus, "The Woodstock Festival," *Rolling Stone*, 20 September 1969.

43. "Woodstock," *Space City News*, 28 August–11 September 1969. (Via Liberation News Service.)

44. Andrew Kopkind, untitled article, *Rolling Stone*, 20 September 1969.

45. John Hilgardt, "That Aquarian Exposition," *East Village Other*, 20 August 1969.

46. "A Murderous Thing," Berkeley *Barb*, 12–18 December 1969.

47. See, for example, George Paul Csicsery, "Stones Concert Ends It," Berkeley *Tribe*, 12–19 December 1969.

48. "Leary Love Rap," Berkeley *Barb*, 26 December 1969–2 January 1970.

49. "A Stony Thing," Berkeley *Barb*, 12–18 December 1969.

CHAPTER 5. THE ETHICS OF COMMUNITY

1. Roy Ald, *The Youth Communes* (New York: Tower, 1970), 140.

2. Rosabeth Moss Kanter, *Commitment and Community: Communes and Utopias in Sociological Perspective* (Cambridge, Mass.: Harvard University Press, 1972), 245.

3. Jules Siegel, "West of Eden," *Playboy* 17, no. 11 (November 1970), 174.

4. Benjamin Zablocki, *The Joyful Community* (Baltimore: Penguin, 1971), 300.

5. Keith Melville, *Communes in the Counter Culture* (New York: William Morrow, 1972), 23.

6. David Satterfield, "Country Music in America (Part III)," *Spectator*, 2 December 1969.

7. "Woodstock," *Space City News*, 28 August–11 September 1969. (Via Liberation News Service.)

8. Greil Marcus, "The Woodstock Festival," *Rolling Stone*, 20 September 1969.

9. Benjamin DeMott, "Rock as Salvation," in White, *Pop Culture in America*, 199–200.

10. Reich, *Greening of America*, 244–245.

11. Chester Anderson, "Notes from the New Geology," San Francisco *Oracle* 1, no. 6 (1967).

12. John Sinclair, "Rock & Roll Dope," *Fifth Estate*, 28 November–11 December 1968.

13. Tuli Kupferberg, "The Coming Catastrophic Age of Leisure," in Joseph Berke, ed., *Counter Culture* (London: Peter Owen Ltd., 1969), 82.

14. John Sinclair, quotation of cover of paper, Berkeley *Tribe*, 17–24 July 1970.

15. Stanley Krippner and Don Fersh, "Communes," *Other Scenes*, October 1970.

16. J. R. Kennedy, "Communes," *Fifth Estate*, 6–19 August 1970.

17. Gene Carlson, "Birth of a Tribe," *Oracle of Southern California*, November 1967.

18. Gorkin, "Notes from New Mexico," *Rag*, 10 July 1969. (Originally published in the *Village Voice*.)

19. William C. Shepherd, "Counter Cultural Religiosity: A Reply to Bellah, Baum, and Lidz," *Sociological Inquiry* 42, no. 2 (1972): 171.

20. Ed Schwartz, "Why Communes Fail," *Fusion*, 12 November 1971, 25.

21. Robert Houriet, *Getting Back Together* (New York: Coward, McCann and Geohegan, 1971), 73.

22. Keith Melville saw the surge of hippies toward communalism as begin-

ning in roughly 1966–1967, arguing that the counterculturists had found both urban life and radical activism wanting by then. See Keith Melville, *Communes in the Counter Culture* (New York: William Morrow, 1972), 22.

23. Mungo, *Total Loss Farm*, 73.

24. Mungo, *Famous Long Ago*, 114.

25. "Fooman Zybar," Washington *Free Press*, 1–15 May 1969.

26. Jan Hodenfield, "It Was Like Balling for the First Time," *Rolling Stone*, 20 September 1969.

27. "Did Mad Moment Mar Beautiful Leary Lecture?" Berkeley *Barb*, 21–27 February 1969.

28. Mungo, *Total Loss Farm*, 99.

29. After many local struggles, Gottlieb deeded Morning Star Ranch to God, helpfully agreeing to continue paying the taxes on it himself. Soon a lawyer went to court to have the ranch attached to satisfy a debt: his client had suffered a lightning loss in Phoenix which had been ruled "an act of God" and therefore not subject to compensation from the insurance company involved. Suddenly, however, God had assets within the reach of the law. See "God Named Party in Property Suits," *Rolling Stone*, 12 July 1969.

30. Steve Haines, "To Build a Nation," Berkeley *Tribe*, 7–13 November 1969.

31. Allen Ginsberg, untitled interview, *Fifth Estate*, 1–15 April 1968.

32. Interview with Timothy Leary, *Yarrowstalks* 00, no. 1 (1967).

33. Schwartz, "Why Communes Fail," 22–23.

34. Stanley Krippner and Don Fersh, "Communes," *Other Scenes*, October 1970.

35. Kit Leder, "Women in Communes," *Win*, 15 March 1970, 14–16. (Originally published in *Women: A Journal of Liberation*.)

36. Vivian Estellachild, "Hippie Communes," *Women: A Journal of Liberation* 2, no. 2 (1970): 43.

37. Marilyn Foster et al., "How We Live as Toads," *Women: A Journal of Liberation* 2, no. 2 (1970): 45.

38. Schwartz, "Why Communes Fail," 24.

39. Quoted in Melville, *Communes*, 49–50.

40. Gene Carlson, "Birth of a Tribe," *Oracle of Southern California*, November 1967.

41. Schwartz, "Why Communes Fail," 25.

42. David E. Smith, "Life with Manson," Berkeley *Barb*, 16–22 January 1970.

43. See, for example, Slater, *Pursuit of Loneliness*, 148.

44. "Talking about My Generation," *Great Speckled Bird*, 15 June 1970.

45. Slater, *Pursuit of Loneliness*, 149–150.

46. Gene Carlson, "Birth of a Tribe," *Oracle of Southern California*, November 1967.

47. Slater, *Pursuit of Loneliness*, 5.

48. Jan Hodenfield, "It Was Like Balling for the First Time," *Rolling Stone*, 20 September 1969.

49. "On the Subject of Music," *Avatar*, 19 January–1 February 1968.

50. Gorkin, "Notes from New Mexico," *Rag*, 10 July 1969. (Originally published in the *Village Voice*.)

51. Mungo, *Total Loss Farm*, 151.

52. Goodman, "The New Reformation," 146.

53. Timothy Leary, "You Are a God, Act Like One," *Mile High Underground*, Fall 1967.

CHAPTER 6. THE ETHICS OF CULTURAL OPPOSITION

1. Cal Steinmetz, "On Bein' at the Be-In," Berkeley *Barb*, 20 January 1967.

2. "Youth: The Hippies," *Time*, 7 July 1967, p. 20.

3. Lionel H. Mitchell, "Look at Down Here," *East Village Other*, 15 June–1 July 1967. Other underground writings strikingly resemble Christian treatises on ideal love; see, for example, "Aquarian Beat," San Francisco *Oracle* 1, no. 6 (1967).

4. Ron Norman, "An Open Letter from One Hippie," *Seventy-Nine Cent Spread*, 5 November 1968.

5. Lionel H. Mitchell, "Look at Down Here," *East Village Other*, 15 June–1 July 1967.

6. Les Wall, "All the Lonely People," *Walrus*, 15–30 October 1968.

7. Tuli Kupferberg, "The Love of Politics and the Politics of Love," Berkeley *Barb*, 12–27 April 1967.

8. Ellen Sander, "Dear Abbie," Los Angeles *Free Press*, 5 September 1969.

9. The Diggers received a great deal of publicity in the early days of the counterculture but then faded from the scene. Some have suggested that only the publicity changed; the term *Digger* fell into disuse, but their activity continued. See Alex Forman and F. P. Salstrom, "Revolution, Diggers Style," *Distant Drummer*, 3–10 October 1969.

10. "Diggers," *Oracle of Southern California*, July 1967.

11. Cal Steinmetz, "On Bein' at the Be-In," Berkeley *Barb*, 20 January 1967.

12. "For Love Not Lucre," Berkeley *Barb*, 25 November 1966.

13. "Just Plain Holy Water," Berkeley *Barb*, 22–28 November 1968.

14. Sam Allen, in a letter to the editor of *Rolling Stone*; quoted with approval in "Quote of the Week," *East Village Other*, 18 February 1970.

15. "Thudpucker Raps," *Dallas Notes*, 2–15 July 1969.

16. "Hippies: Death on a Sunny Afternoon," *Rolling Stone*, 9 November 1967.

17. Jeff Jassen, "Love Community, Conspiracy Clash," Berkeley *Barb*, 10 March 1967.

18. Jeff Jassen, "What Price Love," Berkeley *Barb*, 5–11 May 1967.

19. "Is Love Obscene," Berkeley *Barb*, 26 May–1 June 1967. (Originally published in the *Canadian Free Press*.)

20. Philip Slater wrote that "the fundamental political goal of the new culture is the diffusion of power, just as its fundamental economic goal is the diffusion of wealth." Slater saw such diffusion as both realistic and practical. See Slater, *Pursuit of Loneliness*, 145–47.

21. Mungo, *Famous Long Ago*, 77.

22. Mungo, *Total Loss Farm*, 40.

23. Slater saw that problem as a manifestation of the "compulsive American tendency to avoid confrontation of chronic social problems"—that is, we try "to solve long-range social problems with short-run 'hardware' solutions. . . . Our approach to social problems is to decrease their visibility." See Slater, *Pursuit of Loneliness*, 12, 15.

24. "Roving Rat Fink," Berkeley *Barb*, 3–9 January 1969.

25. Nick Tosches, "Getting Out the Vote," *Fusion*, 26 November 1971, 31.

26. Stan Iverson, "To Touch the Genitals," *Helix* 5, no. 1? (1968).

27. Quoted in Braden, *Age of Aquarius*, 276.

28. Ralph J. Gleason, "Perspectives: Is There a Death Wish in U.S.?" *Rolling Stone*, 5 April 1969.

29. Mungo, *Famous Long Ago*, 168–69.

30. Sun Eagle, "Summer Solstice—New Mexico," *East Village Other*, 10 September 1969.

31. Chester Anderson, "God Works through Harry Anslinger," Los Angeles *Free Press*, 26 April 1968.

32. George Harrison, quoted in Nick Jones, "The Rolling Stone Interview: George," *Rolling Stone*, 10 February 1968.

33. "A Letter Appeal," San Francisco *Oracle* 1, no. 11 (1967).

34. See Paul Scorpio, "LSD and Me (Part II)," *Distant Drummer*, 5–12 February 1970.

35. Reich, *Greening of America*, 7.

36. Yablonsky, *Hippie Trip*, 57.

37. Timothy Leary, "Declaration of Evolution," *East Village Other*, 8 September 1970.

38. Leonard Magruder, "A Middle Aged Beatnik among the Hippies," *Notes from the Underground*, 17–31 January 1968.

39. "Leary and Alpert: Turn On/Tune In/Drop Out," Berkeley *Barb*, 24 June 1966.

40. "Dropouts Delight," San Francisco *Oracle*, January 1967.

41. Clark, *Chemical Ecstasy*, 121–22.

42. Gary Thiher, "Woodstock: Escape from Amerika," *Rag* 3, no. 28 (1969).

43. Lawrence Lipton, "Radio Free America," Los Angeles *Free Press*, 14 August 1970.

44. Alan Watts, "Manifesto to Cut the Big Hang-Up," *East Village Other*, 1–15 January 1968.

45. Alan Watts, "Wealth versus Money," *Playboy* 15, no. 12 (December 1968), 214.

46. Walter Bowart, "Casting the Money Throwers from the Temple," *East Village Other*, 1–15 September 1967.

47. Jerry Rubin, "Rubin Raps: Money's to Burn," Berkeley *Barb*, 19–26 January 1968.

48. Maureen Orth, "Giving $14,905 Away: A Hip Soap Opera," *Village Voice*, 21 October 1971, 5, 8.

49. Mungo, *Total Loss Farm*, 106.

50. Jerry Rubin, "And in America We Are All Learning to Become Vietcong," Berkeley *Barb*, 5–11 January 1968.

51. Kenneth Keniston, *Young Radicals: Notes on Committed Youth* (New York: Harcourt, Brace and World, 1968); quoted in Braden, *Age of Aquarius*, 59.

52. Mungo, *Total Loss Farm*, 105.

53. Neville, *Play Power*, 19.

54. Johan Huizinga, *Homo Ludens: A Study of the Play Element in Culture* (London: Routledge and Kegan Paul, 1949).

55. Neville, *Play Power*, 273–74.

56. *Ibid.*, 274.

57. Ron Jarvis, "When the Mode of the Music Changes," *Space City!* 17–30 January 1970.

58. Allen Ginsberg, "Playboy Interview," *Playboy* 16, no. 4 (April 1969), 240.

59. Abbie Hoffman and Jaakov Kohn, "Abbie," *East Village Other*, 14 May 1969.

60. Slater, *Pursuit of Loneliness*, 46.

61. Reich, *Greening of America*, 242.

62. Neville, *Play Power*, 263.

63. Kupferberg, "Coming Catastrophic Age of Leisure," 85.

64. Slater, *Pursuit of Loneliness*, 103. Slater (p. 97) went so far as to say that scarcity (rather than, say, age) and attitudes regarding it comprised the heart of the difference between the counterculture and majority culture.

65. David Ramsay Steele, "Abolish Money," Washington *Free Press*, 16–31 May 1969.

66. Westhues, *Society's Shadow*, 208.

67. Victor Jasha, "Why Drugs," *Rag*, 27 January 1970.

68. Jerry Rubin, *Do It!* (New York: Simon and Schuster, 1970), 122.

69. Neville, *Play Power*, 269–70.

70. Frank Ferris, "Rip-Off," *East Village Other*, 27 October and 3, 10, and 17 November 1970.

71. See, for example, "Ma Bell Tapped," Berkeley *Tribe*, 31 December 1971–6 January 1972.

72. Abbie Hoffman, *Steal This Book* (New York: Grove, 1971).

73. Brian Kirby, "Yours Truly, Rubber Dubber," Los Angeles *Free Press*, 12 November 1970.

74. Neville, *Play Power*, 18.

75. Jerry Rubin, *We Are Everywhere* (New York: Harper and Row, 1971), 42.

76. Clay Geerdes, "Is Long Hair a Psycho-Sexual Threat to the State?" Los Angeles *Free Press*, 30 May 1969.

77. Thane Gower Ritalin, "The Hippies and the Hypocrites," *Seed*, 11–25 August 1967.

78. Theodore Roszak wrote briefly of the tendency toward cultivation of "a feminine softness" among countercultural males, but, like most other writers, did not pursue androgyny in depth. See Roszak, *Making of a Counter Culture*, 74.

79. Mircea Eliade, *Mephistopheles and the Androgyne* (New York: Sheed and Ward, 1965), 122.

80. *Ibid.*, 110.

81. "Obscenity," Washington *Free Press*, 29 February 1968. (Originally published in the San Diego *Door*.)

82. John Sieler, in *Asterisk* (Omaha), quoted by Ethel Grodzins Romm, *The Open Conspiracy* (Harrisburg, Pa.: Stackpole Books, 1970), 36.

83. Thane Gower Ritalin, "The Hippies and the Hypocrites," *Seed*, 11–25 August 1967.

84. Jean Raisler, "Placid on Acid," Berkeley *Tribe*, 29 August–4 September 1969.

85. Quoted in "High Priest Points Ahead to Happy Era," Berkeley *Barb*, 14–21 February 1969.

86. Quoted in Jean Raisler, "Placid on Acid," Berkeley *Tribe*, 29 August–4 September 1969.

87. "High Priest Points Ahead to Happy Era," Berkeley *Barb*, 14–21 February 1969.

88. Quoted in Phineas Israeli, "The God Game," Berkeley *Barb*, 14–21 February 1969.

89. Quoted in John Wilcock, "Other Scenes," *Fifth Estate*, 27 November–10 December 1969.

90. "Sex Freedom League Aims Clarified," Berkeley *Barb*, 15 April 1966.

91. Leonard Magruder, "A Middle Aged Beatnik Among the Hippies," *Notes from the Underground*, 17–31 January 1968.

92. Braden, *Age of Aquarius*, 17, 258.

93. Paul Krassner (interview), "LSD, Revolution and God," San Francisco *Oracle* 1, no. 6 (1967).

94. Thane Gower Ritalin, "The Hippies and the Hypocrites," *Seed*, 11–25 August 1967.

95. Ralph J. Gleason, "The Final Paroxysm of Fear," *Rolling Stone*, 6 April 1968.

96. Jerry Rubin, "Rubin Raps: Money's to Burn," Berkeley *Barb*, 19–26 January 1968.

97. Abbie Hoffman, quoted in Melville, *Communes in the Counter Culture*, 109.

98. See Braden, *Age of Aquarius*, 159.

99. Roszak, *Making of a Counter Culture*, 205–38.

100. *Ibid.*, 51.

101. Goodman, "New Reformation," 33.

CHAPTER 7. LEGACY

1. Henry Steele Commager, *The American Mind* (New Haven: Yale University Press, 1950), 22.

2. For a history of the "back-to-nature" tradition in America prior to hippie times, see Peter J. Schmitt, *Back to Nature: The Arcadian Myth in Urban America* (New York: Oxford University Press, 1969).

3. *Marihuana: A Signal of Misunderstanding*, 7.

4. John A. O'Donnell et al., *Young Men and Drugs—A Nationwide Survey* (Rockville, Md.: National Institute on Drug Abuse, 1976).

5. Tom Siegfried, "Addiction," *Kansas City Star*, 20 June 1989, T2, (Originally published in the Dallas *Morning News*.)

6. George H. Gallup, *The Gallup Poll* (New York: Random House, 1972), vol. 3, 2216.

7. "The New Morality," *Time*, 21 November 1977, 111–116.

8. Ginsberg, "Playboy Interview," 240.

9. John Gabree, "The System: Venceremos?" *Fusion*, 12 November 1971, 34.

10. Wolfe, *Electric Kool-Aid Acid Test*, 361.

11. Mungo, *Famous Long Ago*, 117–18.

12. "Premarital Sex," *Gallup Report* no. 263 (August 1987): 20–22.

13. "Marijuana Laws," *Gallup Report* no. 241 (October 1985): 28–30.

14. "Opinion Roundup: Societal Indicators," *Public Opinion* 10, no. 4 (November/December 1987): 38–40.

15. Craig Dremann, "Hippie Ethnobotany," *Whole Earth Review* no. 64 (Fall 1989): 25.

16. Kimbrell, "Coming Era of Activism," 66–68.

17. See, for example, Carol Clurman, "More than Just a Paycheck," *USA Weekend*, 19–21 January 1990, 4–5.

18. Roderick Frazier Nash, *The Rights of Nature: A History of Environmental Ethics* (Madison: University of Wisconsin Press, 1989), 166.

19. Rachel Carson, *Silent Spring* (Boston: Houghton Mifflin, 1962).

20. Mark Satin, "Drugs Are Not the Enemy," *New Options* no. 62 (27 November 1989): 1.

21. Siegfried, "Addiction," T1.

22. Jerry Falwell, as quoted by William J. Petersen and Stephen Board, "Where Is Jerry Falwell Going?" *Eternity* 31, no. 7 (July–August 1980): 18–19. Quoted in Jerry Falwell, ed., *The Fundamentalist Phenomenon* (Garden City, New York: Doubleday, 1981), 144.

23. Ingrid Komar, *Living the Dream: A Documentary Study of Twin Oaks* (Norwood, Pa.: Norwood Editions, 1983).

24. Personal communication.

Addendum

Underground Papers Used in This Study

Nearly all of these papers are included in the Bell and Howell Underground Newspaper collection, which consists of 68 rolls of microfilm and covers hundreds of additional titles. *Rolling Stone* is not included in Bell and Howell; I used a complete run in the hands of a private collector. In a very few cases I owned personal file copies of specific issues of papers which had been omitted from Bell and Howell.

American Dream (Tempe)
American Avatar (New York-Boston)
Argus (Ann Arbor)
Avatar (Boston)
Baltimore Free Press
Berkeley Barb
Berkeley Tribe
Big Us (Cleveland)
Buffalo Chip (Omaha)
Connections (Madison)
Daily Planet (Miami)

Dallas Notes; previously, *Notes from the Underground*
Deserted Times (San Francisco)
Distant Drummer (Philadelphia)
Dock of the Bay (San Francisco)
East Village Other (New York)
Fifth Estate (Detroit)
First Issue (Ithaca)
Florida Free Press (Jacksonville)
Good Times (San Francisco); previously, *San Francisco*

Express Times
Great Speckled Bird (Atlanta)
Haight-Ashbury Tribune (San Francisco)
Hair (Minneapolis)
Hartford's Other Voice
Helix (Seattle)
Heterodoxical Voice (Newark, Delaware)
Hips Voice (Santa Fe)
Jabberwock (New York)
Kaleidoscope (Madison)
Kudzu (Jackson, Mississippi)
Los Angeles Free Press
Los Angeles Underground
Middle Earth (Iowa City)
Mile High Underground (Denver)
New Hard Times (St. Louis)
Nola Express (New Orleans)
North Carolina Anvil (Durham)
Northwest Passage (Seattle)
Old Mole (Cambridge)
Open Process (San Francisco)
Oracle of Southern California (Los Angeles)
Other Scenes (New York)
Polar Star (Fairbanks)

Rag (Austin)
Raisin Bread (Minneapolis)
Rat (New York)
Resurrection (Tucson)
Rolling Stone (San Francisco)
San Diego Free Press
San Francisco Oracle
Seed (Chicago)
Seventy-Nine Cent Spread (Carmel, California)
Space City News (Houston); subsequently, *Space City!*
Speak Easy (Attleboro, Massachusetts)
Spectator (Bloomington)
Spokane Natural
Underground Review
Vortex (Lawrence, Kansas, and Kansas City); previously, *Screw*
Walrus (Champaign, Illinois)
Washington Free Press
Willamette Bridge (Portland, Oregon)
Xanadu (St. Louis)
Yarrowstalks (Philadelphia)
Zig Zag (Montague, Massachusetts)

Direct predecessor and successor papers were also used; for example, the *San Francisco Express-Times*, the direct forerunner of the *Good Times*, was used in the study on the same basis as its successor paper.

Bibliography

This bibliography does not include citations of articles from the underground papers used in the study or others from the Bell and Howell Collection (see list above). Those articles are fully cited in the footnotes.

Abramson, H. A., ed. *The Use of LSD in Psychotherapy and Alcoholism.* Indianapolis: Bobbs-Merrill, 1967.

Ald, Roy. *The Youth Communes.* New York: Tower, 1970.

Allegro, John. *The Sacred Mushroom and the Cross.* London: Hodder and Stoughton, 1970.

Banner, Lois W. *Women in Modern America: A Brief History.* San Diego: Harcourt Brace Jovanovich, 2nd ed., 1984.

Berke, Joseph, ed. *Counter Culture.* London: Peter Owen, 1969.

Braden, William. *The Age of Aquarius.* Cleveland: Quadrangle Books, 1970.

Carey, James T. "The Ideology in Popular Lyrics: A Content Analysis." In Kenneth Westhues, *Society's Shadow* (q.v.), 92–110.

Carson, Rachel. *Silent Spring.* Boston: Houghton Mifflin, 1962.

Claiborne, Robert. "Buying Time and Safety: Let's Legalize Heroin." *Village Voice,* 16 December 1971.

Clark, Walter Houston. *Chemical Ecstasy.* New York: Sheed and Ward, 1969.

Clurman, Carol. "More than Just a Paycheck." *USA Weekend,* 19–21 January 1990, 4–5.

Commager, Henry Steele. *The American Mind*. New Haven: Yale University Press, 1950.

Cox, Harvey. "God and the Hippies." *Playboy* 15, no. 1 (January 1968), 93+.

Dedeaux, P. N. "Sade Lib." *Village Voice*, 13 May 1971.

DeMott, Benjamin. "Rock as Salvation." In *Pop Culture in America* (q.v.). Edited by David Manning White, 191–204. Originally published in the *New York Times Magazine*, 25 August 1968.

Dremann, Craig. "Hippie Ethnobotany." *Whole Earth Review* no. 64 (Fall 1989): 25.

Eliade, Mircea. *Mephistopheles and the Androgyne*. New York: Sheed and Ward, 1965.

Estellachild, Vivian. "Hippie Communes." *Women: A Journal of Liberation* 2, no. 2 (1970): 40–41.

Falwell, Jerry, ed. *The Fundamentalist Phenomenon*. Garden City, N.Y.: Doubleday, 1981.

Ferrandino, Joseph. "Rock Culture and the Development of Social Consciousness." *Power to the People: New Left Writings*. Edited by William Slate. New York: Tower, 1970.

Foster, Marilyn et al. "How We Live as Toads." *Women: A Journal of Liberation* 2, no. 2 (1970).

Gabree, John. "The System: Venceremos?" *Fusion*, 12 November 1971, 32–34.

Gallup, George H. *The Gallup Poll*. New York: Random House, 1972.

[Gaskin, Stephen.] *Hey Beatnik! This Is the Farm Book!* Summertown, Tenn.: Book Publishing Co., 1974.

Ginsberg, Allen. "The Great Marijuana Hoax." *Atlantic Monthly* 218, no. 5 (November 1966), 104ff.

———. "Playboy Interview." *Playboy* 16, no. 4 (April 1969), 81+.

Gleason, Ralph J. "Bob Dylan and the Children's Crusade." *Conversations with the New Reality*. Edited by *Ramparts* editors. San Francisco: Canfield Press, 1971.

Goodman, Paul. *New Reformation*. New York: Random House, 1970.

———. "The New Reformation." *New York Times Magazine*, 14 September 1969, 32+.

Gruen, John. *The New Bohemia*. New York: Grosset and Dunlap, 1966.

Hoffman, Abbie. *Steal This Book*. New York: Grove, 1971.

Houriet, Robert. *Getting Back Together*. New York: Coward, McCann and Geohegan, 1971.

Huizinga, Johan. *Homo Ludens: A Study of the Play Element in Culture*. London: Routledge and Kegan Paul, 1949.

Kanter, Rosabeth Moss. *Commitment and Community: Communes and Utopias in Sociological Perspective*. Cambridge: Harvard University Press, 1972.

Keniston, Kenneth. *Young Radicals: Notes on Committed Youth*. New York:

Harcourt, Brace and World, 1968.

Kimbrell, Andrew. "The Coming Era of Activism: New Left Meets New Age." *Utne Reader* no. 26 (March/April 1988): 63–69.

Kleps, Art. *The Boo-Hoo Bible*. San Cristobal, N.M.: Toad Press, 1971.

Kolb, Terry. "Masochist's Lib." *Village Voice*, 13 May 1971.

Komar, Ingrid. *Living the Dream: A Documentary Study of Twin Oaks*. Norwood, Pa.: Norwood Editions, 1983.

Krassner, Paul, and Ken Kesey. "An Impolite Interview with Ken Kesey." *The Realist* no. 90 (May–June 1971): 1, 46–53. Reprinted in *The Best of the Realist*. Edited by Paul Krassner, 213–22. Philadelphia: Running Press, 1984.

Kupferberg, Tuli. "The Coming Catastrophic Age of Leisure." In *Counter Culture*, edited by Joseph Berke (q.v.), 74–87.

Kurland, Albert A. "The Therapeutic Potential of LSD in Medicine." *LSD, Man and Society*. Edited by Richard C. DeBold and Russell C. Leaf, 20–35. Middletown, Conn.: Wesleyan University Press, 1967.

Leamer, Laurence. *The Paper Revolutionaries: The Rise of the Underground Press*. New York: Simon and Schuster, 1972.

Leary, Timothy. *High Priest*. New York: World, 1968.

———. Introduction to *LSD: The Consciousness-Expanding Drug*. Edited by David Solomon, 11–28. New York: G. P. Putnam's Sons, 1964.

———. "Playboy Interview." *Playboy* 13, no. 9 (September 1966), 93+.

———. "The Politics, Ethics, and Meaning of Marijuana." *The Marihuana Papers*. Edited by David Solomon, 121–40. New York: New American Library, 1966.

———. *The Politics of Ecstasy*. New York: G. P. Putnam's Sons, 1968.

———. "The Religious Experience: Its Production and Interpretation." *Journal of Psychedelic Drugs* 1, no. 2 (Winter 1967). Reprinted in *The Psychedelic Reader*. Edited by Gunther M. Weil, Ralph Metzner, and Timothy Leary, 191–213. Secaucus, N.J.: Citadel Press, 1965.

Leary, Timothy, Ralph Metzner, and Richard Alpert. *The Psychedelic Experience*. New Hyde Park, N.Y.: University Books, 1964.

Leder, Kit. "Women in Communes." *Win*, 15 March 1970, 14–16.

Mailer, Norman. *The Armies of the Night*. New York: New American Library, 1968.

———. "The White Negro." *Voices of Dissent*, 197–214. New York: Grove, 1958.

Marihuana: A Signal of Misunderstanding. Official Report of the National Commission on Marihuana and Drug Abuse. New York: New American Library, 1972.

"Marijuana Laws," *Gallup Report* no. 241 (October 1985): 28–30.

Masters, R. E. L., and Jean Houston. *The Varieties of Psychedelic Experience*. New York: Dell, 1966.

McReynolds. "An Open Letter to: Richard Alpert." *Win*, July 1976, 10–12.

Meade, Marion. "Women and Rock: Sexism Set to Music." *Women: A Journal of Liberation* (Fall 1970): 24–26.

Melville, Keith. *Communes in the Counter Culture*. New York: William Morrow, 1972.

Miller, Timothy. "Drug Bust in Kansas." *Christian Century* 88, no. 11 (17 March 1971): 332–33.

Moody, Howard. "Heroin: The Law Is Worse than the Drug," *Village Voice*, 14 September 1972.

Moore, LeRoy, Jr. "From Profane to Sacred America: Religion and the Cultural Revolution in the United States." *Journal of the American Academy of Religion* 39, no. 3 (September 1971): 321–38.

Mungo, Raymond. *Famous Long Ago: My Life and Hard Times with Liberation News Service*. Boston: Beacon, 1970.

———. *Total Loss Farm: A Year in the Life*. New York: Dutton, 1970.

Murphy, Karen, and Ronald Gross. "All You Need Is Love. Love Is All You Need." *Pop Culture in America*. Edited by David Manning White (q.v.), 205–221. Originally published in the *New York Times Magazine*, 13 April 1969.

Nash, Roderick Frazier. *The Rights of Nature: A History of Environmental Ethics*. Madison: University of Wisconsin Press, 1989.

Nederland, Harold. "Asexuals Have Problems Too." *Village Voice*, 25 February 1971.

Neville, Richard. *Play Power*. London: Jonathan Cape, 1970.

"The New Morality," *Time*, 21 November 1977, 111ff.

O'Donnell, John A., et al. *Young Men and Drugs—A Nationwide Survey*. Rockville, Maryland: National Institute on Drug Abuse, 1976.

"Opinion Roundup: Societal Indicators." *Public Opinion* 10, no. 4 (November/December 1987): 21–40.

Orth, Maureen. "Giving $14,905 Away: A Hip Soap Opera." *Village Voice*, 21 October 1971.

Pahnke, Walter N. "Drugs and Mysticism: An Analysis of the Relationship between Psychedelic Drugs and the Mystical Consciousness." Ph.D. dissertation, Harvard University, 1963.

Peck, Abe. *Uncovering the Sixties: The Life and Times of the Underground Press*. New York: Pantheon, 1985.

Perry, Helen Swick. *The Human Be-In*. New York: Basic Books, 1970.

Peterson, William J., and Stephen Board. "Where Is Jerry Falwell Going?" *Eternity* 31, no. 7 (July–August 1980), 18–19. Quoted in *The Fundamentalist Phenomenon*. Edited by Jerry Falwell. Garden City, N.Y.: Doubleday, 1981.

"Premarital Sex," *Gallup Report* no. 263 (August 1987): 20–22.

Reich, Charles. *The Greening of America*. New York: Random House, 1970.

Romm, Ethel Grodzins. *The Open Conspiracy*. Harrisburg, Pa.: Stackpole Books, 1970.

Roszak, Theodore. *The Making of a Counter Culture*. Garden City, N.Y.: Doubleday, 1969.

Rubin, Jerry. *Do It!* New York: Simon and Schuster, 1970.

———. *We Are Everywhere*. New York: Harper and Row, 1971.

Rubin, Sherrie. "Hymens for Husbands." *Everywoman*, 19 June 1970.

Sanders, Ed. *The Family*. New York: Dutton, 1970.

Satin, Mark. "Drugs Are Not the Enemy." *New Options*, no. 62 (27 November 1989): 1.

Schmitt, Peter J. *Back to Nature: The Arcadian Myth in Urban America*. New York: Oxford University Press, 1969.

Schwartz, Ed. "Why Communes Fail." *Fusion*, 12 November 1971, 20–25.

Shepherd, William C. "Counter Cultural Religiosity: A Reply to Bellah, Baum, and Lidz." *Sociological Inquiry* 42, no. 2 (1972): 168–72.

———. "Religion and the Counter Culture—A New Religiosity." *Sociological Inquiry* 42, no. 1 (1972): 3–9.

Siegel, Jules. "West of Eden." *Playboy* 17, no. 11 (November 1970), 174+.

Siegfried, Tom. "Addiction." Kansas City *Star*, 20 June 1989, T2.

Simmons, J. L., and Barry Winograd. *It's Happening*. Santa Barbara: Marc-Laird Publications, 1966.

Slater, Philip N. *The Pursuit of Loneliness: American Culture at the Breaking Point*. Boston: Beacon, 1970.

Smith, Howard. "Scenes." *Village Voice*, 22 April 1971.

Stafford, Peter, ed. *Psychedelic Baby Reaches Puberty*. New York: Praeger, 1971.

Statistical Abstract of the United States, 1972. 93rd ed. Washington: Bureau of the Census, 1972.

Stokes, Geoffrey. "The Sixties." In *Rock of Ages: The Rolling Stone History of Rock and Roll*. By Ed Ward, Geoffrey Stokes, and Ken Tucker, 247–463. New York: Summit Books/Simon and Schuster, 1986.

Tipton, Steven M. *Getting Saved from the Sixties: Moral Meaning in Conversion and Cultural Change*. Berkeley: University of California Press, 1982.

Tosches, Nick. "Getting Out the Vote." *Fusion*, 26 November 1971, 28–31.

Truscott, Lucian K. IV. "Chop, Chop: Age of Psychedelic Fascism." *Village Voice*, 14 October 1971.

Vishner, Mayer. "Rock and Revolution." *Win*, 15 December 1968.

"Warning to So-Called 'Paper Panthers.'" *Black Panther*, 14 September 1968.

Wasson, R. Gordon. *Soma: Divine Mushroom of Immortality*. New York: Harcourt, Brace and World, 1969.

Watts, Alan. "Wealth Versus Money." *Playboy* 15, no. 12 (December 1968), 210+.

Weil, Andrew. *The Natural Mind*. Boston: Houghton Mifflin, 1972.

Westhues, Kenneth, ed. *Society's Shadow: Studies in the Sociology of Countercultures*. Toronto: McGraw-Hill Ryerson, 1972.

White, David Manning, ed. *Pop Culture in America*. Chicago: Quadrangle, 1970.

Wolf, Leonard, ed. *Voices from the Love Generation*. Boston: Little, Brown, 1968.

Wolfe, Tom. *The Electric Kool-Aid Acid Test*. New York: Farrar, Straus and Giroux, 1968.

Yablonsky, Lewis. *The Hippie Trip*. New York: Pegasus, 1968.

"Youth: The Hippies." *Time*, 7 July 1967, 18–22.

Zablocki, Benjamin. *The Joyful Community*. Baltimore: Penguin, 1971.

Index

THE HIPPIES
AND AMERICAN VALUES
was designed by Richard Hendel,
composed by Tseng Information Systems, Inc.,
and printed by Cushing-Malloy, Inc.
The book is set in Baskerville with Gill used for display
and printed on 50-lb Glatfelter Natural.